FACES OF POVERTY

FACES OF POVERTY

Arthur R. Simon

CONCORDIA PUBLISHING HOUSE

St. Louis, Missouri

Concordia Publishing House, St. Louis, Missouri
Concordia Publishing House Ltd., London, E. C. 1
© 1966 by Concordia Publishing House

Library of Congress Catalog Card No. 66-18780

Manufactured in the United States of America

TO MY PARENTS, WHO TAUGHT ME TO CARE

FOREWORD

As for the rich of·this world, charge them not to be haughty nor to set their hopes on uncertain riches, but on God, who richly furnishes us with everything to enjoy. They are to do good, to be rich in good deeds, liberal and generous, thus laying up for themselves a good foundation for the future, so that they may take hold of the life which is life indeed.

1 Timothy 6:17-19 RSV

The service which this book accomplishes is mainly a benefit to the prosperous, not to the poor, although it is a book about the poor.

The virtue of the book is that it exposes the massive indifference of the great multitudes of earnest, sincere-intentioned, church-going, relatively affluent to the humanity of those in American society imprisoned in poverty because they are black or because they are old or because they have no employable or marketable skill. And the book addresses the profound ignorance which lies underneath the insensitivity and apathy of these "good" citizens.

Adult Americans who can remember in their own lifetime the calamity which befell Germany and, shortly after that, the whole world, need now to ponder the efficacy of complacency. Indifference, especially that form of contentment and supposed noninvolvement which is so characteristic of the white American middle and upper classes, achieves results, accomplishes things, and is surely judged by God as seriously as intentional commitment and involvement. Apathy works, even if the social and public consequences of apathy are usually pathetic, and even if the theological meaning of the surrender to apathy be poignant.

This book documents the terrible relationship which inheres at the present time in American society between the ignorance and the moral indifference of most prosperous white Americans to the poor who subsist among them in this land, in which there is far more than enough to spare for everyone to live decently and with dignity and even a little self-esteem.

Part of the problem involved in the apathy of the prosperous has been, as Arthur Simon points out, the anonymity of the poor. The conscience of the white American bourgeoisie is not moved — and cannot reasonably be expected to be provoked to concern and action — by conditions hidden from their apprehension and, for that matter, from their comprehension. This book of Pastor Simon's is most significant at that very point. It takes the reader into some concrete sites of poverty and provides a glimpse into the existential realities of poverty in its peculiar forms in contemporary American society. Thereby the author does the prosperous Americans a distinct service: he remedies their ignorance. If one reads this book, poverty is no longer a matter of statistics, abstraction, or social philosophy, but a matter of flesh and blood: of real human beings who strive and breathe and sleep and think and mourn and love and suffer and fight and catch colds and brush their teeth and change their clothes occasionally. Poverty, as the author himself writes, is people.

But if this book helps to deprive the complacent of their ignorance of the poor as people and therefore of their indifference to the poor as people, it goes beyond, thank God, jeremiad and exhortation. The author has had the wisdom and the grace to come up with some sensible and viable suggestions about how poverty could indeed be banished for this land *if* the nation matures enough to become and be committed to that objective (a matter which unhappily is most pathetically in doubt). The key proposal, expounded in the book, is to *make* work and, most specifically, to create jobs which would gainfully employ those now consigned to poverty and to the humiliating situation of a welfare beneficiary. There is, I am aware, an ideological resistance to this idea, especially among the white, Anglo-Saxon Protestants who have suffered through Sunday school curriculums which indoctrinate the idea that work is intrinsically a virtue and that all forms of occupation or profession must be socially constructive, self-fulfilling, and deeply satisfying. Is this true? The most common form of work in which the middle and upper classes are now engaged in America are forms of *made* work: of jobs created for the sake, chiefly, of creating jobs, and not because the work so conceived and instituted is, in terms of the old Protestant ethic, useful, necessary, or creative. This author suggests that the same principle which governs so much of the employment of middle- and upper-class Americans be now applied to the poor. The idea is no panacea, but it does make sense ethically and it does promise a much more rigorous, imaginative, and realistic assault on the institutionalization of poverty in America than has yet been launched in the so-called war on poverty. If it is good for the goose, let it apply to the poor.

Pastor Simon disclaims in his book that he possesses expertise about poverty. I suppose that may be technically true: he is a clergyman, not a bureaucrat in the Labor Department or a social worker or, as far as I am aware, politically ambitious. But he is a pastor, and this book testifies that he is an authentic pastor in a Christian sense who cares for his people. His people are not just his parishioners, but the human beings he encounters daily, for whom he happens to be given opportunity and responsibility. Those he serves may be anyone and everybody, and his life as a servant means that he could freely die for them, for any one of them, as a servant in Christ.

WILLIAM STRINGFELLOW

The First Sunday in Advent, 1965
New York City

CONTENTS

PREFACE

I have written a book on poverty, not because I can pretend to be
an expert but because I have the frustrating impression that for most
Americans poverty is remote and impersonal. It is urgent,
however, that we see poverty not as a massive problem but as
human suffering. The poor are people; they are people surrounded
by immense difficulties. We who are remote from poverty have
helped to erect those difficulties. We can also help to tear them
down, but we will do so only if we are convinced that the stakes
are high and have to do with flesh-and-blood people. Therefore
I have tried to acquaint you with a few of the people from my
parish on the Lower East Side of Manhattan. They tell their own
stories for the most part. Their names are changed but the people
are real. As nearly as I can determine, the stories are accurate in
every detail. You will of course be led to see these people
through sympathetic eyes.

I am also writing because the poor are speaking an eloquent
word to the church, even though the church isn't listening. The
nature of the church dictates its involvement in human suffering,
and when it is not so involved it betrays itself. In its attitude
toward the poor the church faces the option of being God's
servant in the world or perishing in spite of its abundance — by
becoming a kind of "antichurch." My last chapter deals with
this pressing matter, and although it is a particular word for
those who profess to be Christians, it also speaks, one may hope, to
every man of conscience.

This is a book on poverty in the United States, not on world
poverty. The problem of world poverty is a far more momentous
and an infinitely more disturbing one than poverty in our country.
But I am quite sure that consciences aroused to deal with the poor at
home are less likely to forget the poorer abroad. People who are
apathetic to poverty in their own land are not apt to deal
seriously with it elsewhere. The two walk together.

The book deals primarily with urban poverty. Poverty in rural areas is an immense national sore, to be sure, but the poor I live with are city people, and I am writing about people I know.

I would like to emphasize that this is not an attempt to give a balanced selection of "typical" cases of poverty. The more one sees of the poor the more one realizes that they are much too human to fit their lives into our stereotypes. Poverty has countless faces, and we will not understand the poor by putting a few standardized masks on them. Each instance of poverty has a personality of its own.

I am immeasurably indebted to those who shared themselves so willingly, often suffering through old wounds in doing so. To my surprise none of the people I approached declined to discuss their poverty. With the kind of openness that often characterizes the poor, they wanted to "let people know what it's like to be poor." In fact the idea of writing this book was born in the home of one of the families I describe.

I want to express my gratitude to those who read the manuscript and offered many useful suggestions: Harold Remus of Princeton, N. J.; John Puelle, my colleague at Trinity; my parents; my brother Paul; and Gerry Lohrmann, who also typed the manuscript.

Arthur Simon

FACES OF POVERTY

STRANGERS AND PILGRIMS

When Carl Miller and Eileen Nelson exchanged marriage vows in
a Methodist parsonage on Independence Day 1945, they made a
covenant with poverty.

Carl, 37, was working as a maintenance man in a war plant near
Flushing in New York City. Eileen, 30, worked in a factory that
turned out bullets. Together they brought home $130 a week,
a good income even during the war. Like typical newlyweds, they
were optimistic about the future and thought that their marital
union gave evidence of fine and prosperous years ahead.

Neither of them knew that never again would they come within
striking distance of their wartime wages. Neither realized that in
a short time they would be standing on the sidelines as the prosperity of the postwar world passed them by. They could not guess
that they would become an unwilling part of the massive, impersonal
problem of poverty in America.

The war ended a month after their wedding and both Millers lost
their jobs. Today they and their children belong to the army of the
poor, which our government is marching out to meet in its "war" on
poverty.

The question that insists on intruding is "Why?" Why were the
Millers swallowed up by poverty? Why were they unable to claim
a decent share in the expanding wealth of the richest nation on
earth? The usual answers testify falsely and bewitch us with a sense
of moral aloofness that evades the real problem of poverty in
America today. Contrary to widely accepted myths about poor
people the Millers were not shiftless, dishonest, or immoral. They
did not even carry the stigma of color. They had no desire to
freeload on the public. They wanted to work. Yet they were drawn
into poverty much like a drowning man is drawn into the vortex of
a whirlpool.

I first met the Millers on a hot summer day in 1962 as I was
standing on the steps of our parish house. A family walked by
along East Ninth Street and I greeted them. The father was tall,

gaunt, and graying. His head was slightly bowed and also turned, concealing the fact that one of his eyes was sunken. His wife was small and thin, but with lively eyes. A slender boy of about 15 years stood with them, and a small, blond girl no more than 5. Mrs. Miller returned my greeting and they stopped to talk.

Later I visited them in their dingy 4-room apartment, and during the next year I saw them a few times on the street. It wasn't until the summer of 1963 that one of our young parish workers helped me get to know the family well. By pounding up and down three flights of tenement stairways dozens of times, bringing food supplies or clothes, agonizing with Eric about going to school or working, getting Susan to the hospital — from one crisis to the next — we began to learn their story.

Carl Miller was born in the Bronx on Jan. 9, 1908. His father operated a private taxi firm called "Miller Cab Company" and seemed to do well in the business.

Carl had a good relationship with his three younger sisters and his mother but not with his father. "My father was no good. He was mean to my mother and didn't spend any time with me and my sisters. I was always upset because he came home and would carry on. My mother had to take care of everything. He was useless." His father liked to drink and gamble, a liking that increased over the years.

Carl did not do well in school. "Five years I went to an ungraded class for kids who couldn't catch up on certain subjects. I was okay in reading and spelling but no good in math. I never could get math.

"When I was 14 my father saw an ad in the paper on 'Trea-sureland Homes' [then a suburban development in Bayside, New York City]. He bought three homes. He rented two of them and we moved into the third. I liked it in Bayside. I didn't mind going to school, and after school I had delivery jobs."

Then came a setback that was to torment him the rest of his life. "I was going down the front steps of the house. Some boys were on the street shooting small brass staples at each other with rubber bands. One of them hit me in the left eye. It was an accident.

I didn't know how bad it was. I went to school the next day, but
the teacher sent me to the hospital. At the hospital they told me
they would have to take my eye out, so they took it out the next
day. It was a big shock to me."

When Carl was 16 he was sent to a state school for the emotionally
disturbed in upstate New York, where he spent two years. At first
he didn't like it and ran away twice, but then he changed his
mind. "I decided I wasn't getting anywhere running away, so
I settled down. It was a beautiful place out in the country,
and it helped me. It calmed my nerves and did me a world of good.

"When I came home I got jobs cleaning yards and making deliv-
eries. Everybody knew me," he remembers. For the next 15 years,
through the heart of the Depression, Carl worked on a number of
jobs, but he always worked. He worked cutting and laying sod
around new homes on Long Island. He worked as a watchman for
Whitestone Wreckers. He did cleaning work in several taverns.
"They liked me because I didn't drink." Then during the war he got
the job as a maintenance man for Sperry Gyroscope, a firm that
made parts for guns. Carl earned $90 a week take-home pay.

Carl Miller was 36 when he met Eileen Nelson.

She was born in Woodhaven, Queens, in 1914. Her father,
Alfred Nelson, was a bank teller at the time, but when she was
about eight, he formed a real estate business with two other men
in Flushing. He did well in real estate, even during the
Depression.

Eileen, born with curvature of the spine, was inclined to be a
sickly child. "I was delicate and nervous," she observed. "When
I turned 10, my spine began to bother me, and I was transferred to
a small private school."

"We were a very close family," she recalls. "My parents were
devoted. They did things together. My father would set me on his
lap and read stories to me and take me on the sled. He was tender
and kind." The only other child in the family was a brother,
Alfred, five years older than Eileen.

"When I was 18 my mother died. My brother Alfred got married
just before Mother's death, and he had me and my father move
into their home in College Point [in Queens, not far away]. We

lived there eight miserable years. Alfred and his wife didn't get
along, and she took it out on me. I wanted to move into my own
apartment, but my father wouldn't hear of it, so I stayed.

"I began working after my mother died. First I worked in College
Point making baskets, then in a Long Island City [Queens] candy
company. I took candy off a conveyor belt and boxed it. I did
well, so they put me in charge of eight girls, and I earned $45
a week, but after a year I quit. I was all worn out being over
those girls.

"Then I worked for a few years in a dress shop selling dresses
and fitting hats, but I got tired of selling. I got a job taking
care of some children two blocks from where we lived. I liked that
job a lot, but when we moved to Great Neck [Long Island], I had
to quit." The war was now on and Eileen got a job with Tecna
Plastic, which manufactured bullets. "I worked 50 hours a week
for $40. All this time I wanted my own home, and I kept asking,
'When is my own life going to begin?'

"Carl and I met in the Greyhound bus terminal lunch counter in
Flushing, next to my father's real estate office. He was always nice
to me, never fresh. I never had to be afraid. He was kindly and
I could tell he really cared. We both had suffered, and we understood each other.

In August 1945, a month after the Millers were married, Japan
surrendered, and wartime contracts were canceled. Both Millers
found themselves out of work.

Mr. Miller got employment as a dishwasher and pot-cleaner in
Flushing at $36 a week—quite a letdown. During the next half year
he had two other dishwashing and mopping jobs. He would quit and
try to find better employment, but without success, until he was down
to working in a spaghetti plant for $20 a week.

During these months living accommodations were a problem. The
Millers began their married life in an attic. Then they were able
to secure two furnished rooms for $21 a week, but the expense
made it unbearable—especially when Mr. Miller was earning $20
a week in the spaghetti plant.

"We saw an ad in a newspaper about the Sanford Towers. It was
a big apartment house on Union Street. Carl worked there as a

porter and fireman for about seven months. We got two rooms and
a bath in the basement, plus $50 every two weeks. I was carrying
Eric and going around in men's trousers helping Carl. The people
in the house were friendly to us and gave us some food and baby
clothes. We liked it there, but the superintendent began pestering
me, so we decided to move," Mrs. Miller said.

The Millers found themselves caught in a web of circumstances
they could not understand or control. They wanted desperately
to improve themselves, but after the war it was not easy for
a man with a glass eye and no skills. They felt rootless and
frustrated and sometimes thought that any change would be a
chance to get ahead.

After a couple of unsatisfactory dishwashing jobs, Mr. Miller got
a job at a restaurant as a busboy and dishwasher at $30 a week,
working nights. The job lasted a year. "I was laid off because all
the employees had to take a physical exam, and I had varicose
veins. They didn't bother me then though."

The Millers were able to manage on $30 a week, although they
were paying $15 a week rent. "We lived on 'Bum's Hill.' That was
my name for it," she said. "We called it 'Bum's Hill' because it
had nothing but that kind of people — the worst women and the
worst men. We couldn't wait to get out." But Mrs. Miller had only
two months to go with Eric, so they waited.

Eric was born in Aunt Esther's house in Queens Village July 7,
1946. The plan was to have the baby at Aunt Esther's home with
a doctor in attendance. Eric arrived before the doctor did.

"The doctor just checked me and gave me some sleeping pills,
but I threw them away. When Carl came there was still the after-
birth, and he cleaned it all up. It didn't faze him a bit.
I always felt better when he was near.

"We moved from 'Bum's Hill' and for the next six months lived
in the cellar of my father's real estate office. Dad had put some
old furniture there after my mother's death, and so we fixed up
the cellar to live in. There were no windows, but the rooms were
big," Mrs. Miller recalls.

"Finally we got a place on Union Street, three rooms in an old
building. The rent was $40 a month. We lived there $4\frac{1}{2}$ years."

Shortly after they moved to Union Street, Mr. Miller was able to find better employment. He secured work at a restaurant on Manhattan's west side as a dishwasher and cleanup man for $45 a week. Situated above it was a machine shop.

"After two months I got a job in the machine shop for $55 a week sweeping floors and running envelopes through a machine. I had that job for nearly five years. Then I had to leave," Mr. Miller says. "They wanted me to stay. I was worried about getting another job, so I stayed as long as I could; but my veins were popping out, and my legs swelled up so bad I had to quit."

About two years before Mr. Miller quit his job at the machine shop the Millers moved from their home in Flushing to the west side of Manhattan. In doing so they were opting for an oppressive, nomadic style of life that would saddle them with incredible difficulties. They had no way of knowing this, however. They moved for several reasons. First of all, word got around that the buildings in their area were going to be torn down because they were dilapidated, and the Millers had no reason to expect that the new buildings would be erected for their income level. A more pressing reason, however, was the same thing that draws most people into the heart of the city—work. They wanted to get closer to Carl's machine shop. "The job wore me out, and the long trip home standing on a crowded train didn't do me any good. I hoped that by moving close to the machine shop I could keep on working there." That hope turned out to be short-lived. This was in 1951, and Eric was five years old.

The Millers left their apartment with whatever possessions they could carry, took the subway to Manhattan, and got a newspaper to see what was advertised. They went to a hotel on West 49th Street and saw a room for $23 a week. The room looked so bad that they walked out. The Millers didn't know what to do next, so they asked a taxicab driver. He took them to a place on 8th Avenue and 47th. They were there about four months.

Mr. Miller tells it this way: "The manager was nice. He would give us the shirt off his back. But he had a bum crowd. Transient men and women. Not Bowery bums, but people who didn't live like

we do. We had one room and a bath for $21 a week, but it was
a terrible room, and we had to eat out."

The hotel "office" is above a corner bar. The stairs are squeaky,
the halls are unbelievably narrow. The wood and furnishings seem
to exude 19th-century air. The rooms are tiny, and toilet facilities
shared. There are dozens of small, cheap hotels like this west of
Times Square in the vicinity of the machine shop where Carl
worked, and the Millers were due to get acquainted with many
of them in short order.

For the next five months they tried a succession of such hotels,
but always with the same frustration. "We wanted to settle down
and live like ordinary folks, but to get an apartment you need
to pay a month's rent and a month's security. We never had enough
money for that, and we didn't want to beg from anybody. We
wanted to make it on our own. We had a little pride," Mr. Miller
said.

The Marie Antoinette on West 63d Street became an oasis for
a year. There they had two funished rooms and a bath for $25
a week — nearly half of Carl's salary. The contrast between this
and the places they had been staying made them happy. "There
were wonderful people there. It was one of the nicest hotels
in New York. Carl was working, and I could keep my head up,"
Mrs. Miller recalls. They were stalling off the inevitable, however.
Mr. Miller's feet and legs got so bad he had to quit his job at the
machine shop. Since he was unemployed, there was no way for
them to pay the rent, and the hotel manager advised them to go
on welfare. That was in 1953.

"We would have none of it," she insisted. "Instead, we found
a hotel on Ninth Avenue near Times Square that offered a room for
$14 a week. Carl was getting an unemployment check of $45
a week. It was a wretched place."

In the meantime Mr. Miller got in touch with Jimmy Phillips,
a man for whom he had worked as a watchman four years before
his marriage. Phillips was then supervisor of a large ware-
house building on 43d Street between 11th and 12th Avenues.
He knew and respected Carl and got him started on a 2-days-
a-week job, and gradually over a period of four months worked

it up to a regular 5-days-a-week job. In the meantime the Millers
made it by squeezing pennies and eating their main meal each
day at a Salvation Army center. The meals cost 20 cents apiece.
Even so, once they were so broke that they left the hotel and
slept for a few nights on some potato sacks in the loft of the
building where Carl worked. Phillips gave the Millers some money
for food over the weekend until their check came.

"We had a roof over our heads, we had a bite to eat, and
somebody cared," said Mrs. Miller, laughing. "'Well, we're
all together,' Carl would say. He always felt that way. As long
as we were together that was the most important thing. So
I didn't mind sleeping on burlap bags or eating hamburgers.
But I couldn't do it with any other kind of man."

Before long Mr. Miller was working a 7-day week for Phillips
and making $87 take-home pay. He was a watchman, but did odd
jobs as well. With this income they were able to break the cycle
of cheap hotels and get a furnished apartment on West 45th Street
in Hildona Court, where they lived for four years. Two rooms and
a bath cost them $28 a week. Why didn't they try to get a normal,
unfurnished apartment? "We should have, but we just couldn't save
money," Mrs. Miller explained. "It would mean going back to the
cheap hotels for a while, and I was very nervous. I just couldn't
take it anymore. I always had to worry about the people in those
hotels, and sometimes tell somebody off. I had to have a Bible in
one hand and a boxing glove on the other." Emotionally weary,
the Millers found temporary refuge from the world in their new
quarters.

On July 18, 1957, about three years after the Millers came to
Hildona Court, Susan was born at the Polyclinic Hospital. To
finance the new arrival, the Millers took out a $300 loan from
a finance company at an inflated rate of interest.

Eric was eight years old when the Millers moved into Hildona
Court. Since they were moving around so much, or expecting to
move, Eric's mother taught him to read a little and to count,
but he had never gone to school. In the lobby of the hotel they
met Mrs. Price, a retired schoolteacher who was disabled. She asked
if she could teach Eric privately, so for more than three years he

had a private tutor in Mrs. Price. Eric liked her and ran errands for her in exchange. Even after she was bedridden she continued to teach Eric.

In 1959 the Millers received another jolt. United Parcel purchased the property of the block between 11th and 12th Avenues where Carl worked. Less than two years after Susan was born, wreckers came and demolished the buildings and, along with the buildings, Carl's job.

"Jimmy Phillips wanted to help us," said Mr. Miller, "so he talked to the foreman of Associated Wreckers and told them not to hire a watchman because I was a good one. For 10 weeks, while the wreckers were working, I stayed on at the same pay. When the building was level, I talked to the foreman about getting a job, but there were no openings. I tried over and over to get a job as a watchman, but nobody would hire me."

Mrs. Price wanted them to contact Mrs. Miller's brother, who was managing a nursing home in Florida. She refused, so Mrs. Price phoned him on her own. "Are you going to send money?" she asked. He sent them $20 with a letter in which he wrote, "God helps those who help themselves." Mrs. Miller said she wasn't angry but felt sorry that her own brother didn't understand. "Sometimes you can't help yourself," she wrote him. She felt lost.

Mrs. Price sent Mr. Miller to "Big Joe," the announcer on "The Happiness Exchange" radio program. "He helped lots of people," said Carl. "We used to listen to his program. People whose homes were burned out or who were in accidents would be on the program, and people would send in money. But he told me our case wasn't bad enough for his program, and he told us to go on welfare." Mrs. Price had been suggesting welfare too, but the Millers had resisted it until now. Welfare stamps you as a failure, and people think you are lazy. But now they had no choice, so the Millers became a welfare case.

"When Carl lost his job he got $45 a week unemployment, so we had already moved into a small hotel again," said Mrs. Miller. "Then a welfare investigator found a place for us in the West Village [lower Manhattan], an apartment facing the waterfront. It was three small rooms on the fourth floor of an old tenement.

The rent was $90 a month. From the window you could see the cars going by on the West Side Highway. Welfare helped us out with an $80 check for furniture, but we had to wait for the check. We slept three nights on the floor." Susan was now about 2 and Eric 12.

It was a much better home than the cheap hotels they had been living in. It was also a sign of defeat, a sign that society would help them exist but would not permit them the self-respect of working.

"We moved into the West Village in December of 1960, just a few weeks before Christmas. We were waiting for the next unemployment check, but it didn't come. We began to panic. We went around the corner to Benny's grocery store and explained. He let us take $40 worth of groceries on credit. It was like an old home town in the country there. Benny was good to us. But no check came the next week either, or the next. Marie, the woman behind the counter in Benny's, took up a collection of $17 to help us. Then the police came with a Christmas tree and toys for the children. Some ladies from a church gave us things. It was three weeks before the checks came, all three at once! Nobody knew what we went through." That was two days before Christmas.

Eric began public school when the Millers moved to the West Village. "It was a bad school, a lot of gangs," Eric explained. "A lot of kids went into the '600 schools' [for problem children] from there. Sometimes the kids would hit the teachers. The teachers had no control. The kids were like a pack of animals. They would throw things at the teachers." Eric remembers that this was espe-cially true in a shop class with one teacher they disliked. "They threw boards and tools at him. They broke vises and windows and pulled down his bulletin boards. They ransacked his closet and sometimes tried to punch him one. He had some court cases going, he told me. He said he had it easier when he taught in Harlem. The school had lots of Negroes and Puerto Ricans, but the white kids were just as bad. Most teachers had better control than he did. Maybe they were afraid and tried not to show it. He was afraid."

Eric didn't like the school, but he did all right in his studies.

He learned the hard way that New York City, like other cities, offers the worst schools to the poor.

In September of 1961 the Millers decided to get off welfare. They still had three months to go on unemployment checks, plus $175 returned to them from income tax payments. They hoped that this sum, plus unemployment checks, would give them enough time for Carl to get a job. So they told the investigator, and they were dropped immediately.

It was a mistake. "We knew we couldn't pay $90 a month rent," Mrs. Miller explained, "so we found a place close by on Bleecker Street, two tiny rooms and a bath for $32 a month. With the $175 we were able, for the first time, to lay out two months' rent.

"It was six flights up. It was the worst building we ever lived in. The day we moved in Eric fell through a broken fire escape to the fifth floor fire escape, and we had to take him to the hospital. There were beatniks and women next door, dope parties, and bums sleeping on the roof. The stairs and the hallways were crumbling, the plaster was falling down.

"By Christmas we were down almost to nothing again, and Carl couldn't find a job. The man who ran a delicatessen across the street gave us some food. The police helped us out too. So did some people from Our Lady of Peace. All along we met people who cared. God cared for us, and He used people to do it. Sometimes we were frightened, but somebody always came along and helped.

"When we were down to nothing we had to go back to welfare. At welfare they told us we should have come sooner, but I can't keep something in my bag and go to welfare."

While the Millers were on welfare, Mr. Miller would report for job openings to the welfare rehabilitation center on the Lower East Side, a short distance across town on lower Manhattan. "Sometimes they called me in every week or every other week, sometimes every day. They'd send me out to apply for jobs all over the city. Sometimes the places would make me take exams. Sometimes I just filled out application forms when I applied. Usually they sent me out for jobs I just couldn't handle. It was crazy. Others would be there to apply for the same job, and the younger men always got 'em."

This proved to be a discouraging ordeal for Mr. Miller. His vision and his varicose veins were against him. So were his age, his lack of education, and his work record. By this time he knew very well that few employers considered him employable, and each trip was a humiliating reminder of that fact. Mr. Miller had often been job hunting on his own, but with constant rejection, and it was also an expensive undertaking because of the travel fare and meals involved.

In April 1962 Mrs. Miller found a 4-room apartment on the 600 block of East 13th Street, not far from the rehabilitation center. Since they were illegally crowded in their Bleecker Street apartment, welfare gave them permission to move, although the rent was $90 a month. They put the pieces of furniture they had acquired on a truck, and for $12 moved to East 13th Street.

"Welfare promised us $85 for furniture, but it took three months for the check to get there," said Mr. Miller. "Eric and I brought in furniture off the street—chairs, a couch, a bed and mattresses, two armchairs, a desk, some lamps and bookcases, and a rocking chair for Susan. We painted them at home. Most of the stuff they throw out on the street is worthless," he explained, "but we hunted until we got things that weren't so bad." The Millers were then able to use most of the $85 for living expenses.

It was while the Millers were on 13th Street that I met them. They lived there for a year and a half. Like most old tenements, it left a lot to be desired. The building was not well kept. It had strong odors and was noisy. "The children on the street broke open mailboxes. Strangers came into the building all the time. Maybe they were peddling dope," Mrs. Miller suggested. "There were a lot of fires in the building, and that scared us. The lady who lived below us with her children sometimes fought with the men who came to see her, and we didn't want to have any of it. Then, when Eric was bitten by termites from the closet and had to go to Bellevue for treatment, we decided we had enough. So for weeks we went up and down the streets looking for a better place. We found a 3-room apartment on 10th Street. Since the rent there was cheaper, welfare was happy to let us move."

Here the Millers have lived since September 1963—on a $100.60

check twice a month, paying $62.00 a month for rent.

That leaves them $138 a month for food and other expenses. Although welfare may give an emergency allotment for clothing or furniture, the Millers' regular checks still amount only to $1.16 a day per person for ordinary living expenses — which is less than most of us spend for food alone.

Since going on welfare early in 1962, Mr. Miller has had two part-time jobs. For six months he worked at the Men's Shelter on East Third Street. The Men's Shelter is a city-owned building near the Bowery which feeds 2,000 to 2,500 derelicts every day, and until recently housed 580 of them each night. It isn't a pretty place. Mr. Miller waited on these pitiable men from behind the counter. "I gave them coffee and soup and sandwiches. I worked five days a week from 1 to 5 p. m. and earned $1.45 a day. They let me keep it and didn't take it off the welfare check. It wasn't much, but it helped. I liked the work. Then a rash broke out on my face and neck, and I was let go. They told me I could have the job back when my face cleared. After a few months, when my face cleared, I went back, but they told me the job had been taken by someone else. I tried three times to get the job back." It still upsets Mr. Miller.

He also worked for one day a week for about half a year in a garment factory, sweeping floors and cleaning toilets. Most of the workers there were women, and they made ladies' and children's pajamas. "It was filthy work. They didn't have the proper equipment, and I had to pick up dirt from the ladies' rooms by hand. I made $9.72 a week, and welfare let me keep it. Then I got those terrible skin sores around my lips. They began to swell, and I was ashamed to let anybody see me. I think I picked up the skin infection at work."

Even part-time work can make a big difference for a family on welfare. It can give a man a sense of being useful.

Ever since Mr. Miller was 14 and had his left eye removed, he wore a glass eye. Although a glass eye doesn't help anyone's vision, it does wonders for one's appearance and morale. Glass eyes are also easy to break when you take them out to wash them. While the Millers were at Bleecker Street, Mr. Miller broke his

glass eye. "I contacted our welfare investigator about it, but
while I was waiting I got an infection in my eye. I had to go to
the Polyclinic Hospital to have a little surgery done, and have it
cleaned and drained. My eye socket took about three weeks to heal,
and I had to go to the hospital several times a week for a treatment. Then the hospital gave me a slip for welfare for a new eye.
They told me to get the slip to welfare right away and get the
glass eye as fast as possible, because the eye socket was starting
to shrink and close up. I sent the slip to them, but didn't hear
anything. I started to worry and called them up. They told me
I would have to have a special form. I went to the hospital,
but there they told me their slip was okay. About a month went by,
and by this time the hole had partially closed, and all I could be
fitted for was a 'baby eye.'" The eye is, in fact, so small it can
hardly be seen. His left eye is sunken, almost completely shut, and
constantly drains pus.

This problem is further complicated by the fact that Mr. Miller's
vision is failing in his right eye. He has to use a magnifying
glass to read. He was fitted with glasses once by welfare, but the
frames were purple and looked like ladies' glasses. The time and
the red tape involved in getting glasses from welfare is also discouraging. ("What you have to go through to get a pair of
glasses!") Besides, Mr. Miller doesn't think the glasses helped him
much, so he settles for a magnifying glass.

It's not that welfare is unwilling. Welfare has suggested that
the Millers have their teeth fixed—which in Mr. Miller's case means
pulled. After the incident with the glass eye, however, they are
afraid. "I can't go through with it. I'd be a nervous wreck.
I wouldn't have any teeth. I can eat meat now, so I'm doing all
right."

Like most people on welfare, the Millers have mixed feelings
about it. At times they speak of welfare as a friend and bene-
factor. At other times it bears for them the stigma of failure.
("Thank God we hadn't heard of welfare! We were on our own!")
At best, the red tape and impersonal nature of welfare is a source
of irritation, and at worst it is dehumanizing. About welfare
investigators Mrs. Miller says, "What grisly men! But some of them

are nice. They're better now. They used to be bad. We had seven or eight of them when we were on 13th Street. Every couple of weeks a new one. Then we had to go through the whole story all over again!"

Living on welfare can be complicated.

When Susan was born the Millers borrowed $300 from a finance company, and paid back the loan at the rate of $11 a month. However, when Mr. Miller lost his watchman's job and the family went on welfare, they were unable to continue payments. As a matter of fact, persons on welfare are told not to make such payments and are legally protected against their creditors. Nevertheless, in 1964 the finance company began harassing the Millers for payment, first by direct visits, then by resorting to methods like leaving notes scribbled: "It has arrived! Please phone _____." Or: "Call _____! It's an emergency!" The phone number would reach a loan collector. Then they harassed the neighbors and embarrassed the Millers. They also threatened to take away their furniture. Welfare told the Millers to stand firm, but they relented.

Early in the summer of 1964 the Millers had their gas and electricity turned off, and kept it off for four months. Their idea was to give the loan company the amount they saved. It turned out to be a painful and expensive way to save money.

First of all, in order to heat any food they had to buy cans of Sterno for 45 cents a can. Sterno is the stuff campers sometimes use for cooking out — and also the kind of stuff Bowery transients sometimes drink as a cheap intoxicant. But Sterno is not meant for regular cooking. "You can't boil a pot of potatoes on Sterno," said Mrs. Miller. There was also added expense because they couldn't keep food in the refrigerator, and so food was always rotting. The food bill mounted.

Cockroaches are a classic annoyance on the Lower East Side, but spoiling food on hot summer days is an invitation to invasion. The cockroaches invaded. Eric used to sweep his little room carefully at night to make sure his bed was brushed clean before retiring.

Since they had no light, the Millers bought small candles, four for a nickel, and used a dozen of them each night. Eric often read by candlelight.

Poverty takes its toll on children too. Eric and Susan are no exceptions.

Eric remembers his childhood as a happy one, particularly because the family was together so much. But there was also the moving around. "I worried about it. I was afraid it would keep on and on. It made me feel unsettled. It was a crazy, mixed-up situation. You were never able to settle down and concentrate on anything." Sometimes he worried, too, about not going to school. He wanted to go, yet was afraid of it. Not going made him a "loner," even after he started attending school. "The one close friend I remember is a Spanish boy, Jose Hernandez, who lived on MacDougal Street when we lived on Bleecker. We used to walk back and forth to school. We visited each other's homes and would go to movies together."

Eric is also sorry he didn't go on to high school. "I'd be crazy if I wasn't," he says. "But I heard so much about Seward High — teachers, all kinds of things. They said it was worse than Junior High. Lots of gangs." Eric realizes now that these fears were greatly exaggerated, but says that wasn't the main reason anyway. "We were on welfare, and things weren't going so good. It takes money — books, bus fare, and you have to wear decent clothes. Besides, I was older. So I hoped I might get a job." But 16-year-old school dropouts do not get jobs.

Eric soon realized that his chances of landing a job before he turned 18 were virtually nil, so he began to amuse himself. "I often went for long walks and saw parts of Manhattan. I looked in store windows. I watched skaters at Rockefeller Plaza. I took in free television shows and got autographs from famous people, and sometimes I went to a movie. At home I listened to the radio a lot and read newspapers, teen-age magazines, mysteries, and biographies. I was pretty content."

Once he started a correspondence course through some Los Angeles school he saw advertised. It cost $10 a month, and at first he was enthusiastic, but soon lost interest and dropped it.

He sent his name in to *Teen Screen* magazine. It was printed in a pen pal's column, and Eric got an avalanche of mail. It was exciting. Over 200 letters came in within a month, mostly from girls, and Eric sorted out the best ones and began replying. "I got to meet new people that way from all over the world. I got to learn their likes and dislikes. It gave me something to do." It was an escape from reality, but Eric thinks it did him good.

When he turned 18, the welfare rehabilitation center sent him to a job placement service that gives special attention to school dropouts from welfare families. He was sent by them to JOIN (Job Orientation in Neighborhoods), a city job-training program for youth. Here he worked for $20 as a stock boy. Eric had the impression when he started that he would get periodic raises and that the job would develop into a regular position, neither of which was true. The value of establishing a work record and work habits didn't mean much to Eric, so he got discouraged after a month and quit. "I'd be out of a job anyway, when I was through, or else I'd be a stock man all my life."

The agency sent him out for several other jobs that failed to materialize, but then he got a delivery job. He was to report for work on a Monday morning and bought himself a new pair of shoes for the job. Over the weekend he broke in his new shoes walking around at the World's Fair and got badly blistered feet. He neither phoned in nor reported for work until Wednesday, and by that time someone else had the job. The agency was disappointed. Welfare dropped Eric from benefits, which reduced the family allotment. "I felt rotten. I was disgusted with welfare and disgusted with myself." After trying unsuccessfully to get a job on his own, Eric was willing to cooperate with the agency again, and welfare reinstated him. But Eric is still out of work.

What about the future for Eric? "I don't think it looks bad. I think there are lots of opportunities. I'm not worried. I think the worst thing would be to feel defeated. Sometimes I feel that way, but I try to snap myself out of it." Eric says he wants to finish high school, maybe through night school and part-time work.

Eric has a lot in his favor. He has an understanding of suffering, a good mind, and he is honest.

He also has a lot against him — a pattern of letting time and opportunities slip by. Eric once said about the crises his family has been through, "There was always somebody like a hero who

rushed in to help us; somebody would come and save the ship."
His involvement in poverty could be an enriching experience. The
danger is that Eric may drift along, subconsciously waiting for
someone to rush in and save the ship, and then one day realize he
has become a second-generation prisoner of poverty.

The wound of Susan is young but deep.

Susan is abnormally attached to her mother. Most of her life
she has refused to do anything unless her mother is constantly with
her. The world to her is a frightening world, and she doesn't want
to grow up. She gave up her bottle at five — her mother couldn't take
it away before then. When the time came for Susan to go to kindergarten, she threw tantrums, so the Millers decided to drop the
idea. She was enrolled in the first grade at the age of seven, but
ran home the first day. She was afraid of school. After a visit
by a truant officer and a social worker, and a few questions from
friends who visited, Susan withdrew more and more. She refused to
go to church or any place where she might have to talk to someone.
Soon she began screaming and slamming doors when friends came
to the home. Susan is now in the children's psychiatric division of
Bellevue Hospital, an emotionally ill girl who is responding to
professional care.

"There were a lot of sorrows, the way we lived," Mrs. Miller
reflects. "We never should have gone to all those hotels. We needed
an anchor." Mr. Miller agrees. "We had a rough life, but we thank
God He took us through it together. We had a lot of happiness
along the way."

The most impressive strength of the Millers is their faithfulness
to each other, which held them together through crisis after crisis.

"We give each other a lot of understanding and affection," says
Mr. Miller. "I needed her companionship."

"Carl was always good about money," she reflects. "He never
complained about anything. He was always satisfied with the food
we had. As his mother used to say, 'He's not smart, but he's a good
man!' He cared about me. He worried when I was sick. He rubbed
my back when it was sore." Mrs. Miller still has old birthday
cards and love notes from Mr. Miller, and yellowed clippings of
sentimental verses from the newspapers that he used to read to her.

"Even when we didn't have a penny, he would surprise me with something, even if it was only a card or a vase somebody had thrown away. It may have been worthless to them, but to me it meant a lot. We always stuck together. We never forgot we were man and wife. We sometimes got out the marriage certificate and reminded ourselves that we were going to stick together no matter what, and we did. It wasn't easy, but we did."

Although he doesn't mention it often — he is the "silent sufferer," as Eric describes him — not being able to work is demoralizing for Mr. Miller and for the family. "I've worked since I was 14," he says. "I wasn't lazy. I got a lot of satisfaction out of my work. It kept my mind occupied and I was able to take care of my family. I always wanted to work. There are so many that want to work and can't get work. There are a lot of people in the same situation, and they can't get work either. I still want to work."

Wanting to work is not enough, however. More than we may care to admit, ours is a society in which the fit survive, and our notion of fitness is often irrational and morally deficient. In many respects the Millers measured up. They were white, and both came from middle-class families. They grew up in a world which expected them to make their way, and they were determined to do just that. But life became something like a whirlpool for them. Poor health and lack of skills sucked them to the bottom. And now the specter of second-generation poverty haunts the Miller children, who are prepared by hurt to face society's increasingly stringent demands.

Even today, though he is 57 years old, unskilled and handicapped, there are socially useful jobs Mr. Miller could do to make himself and his family feel worthwhile, but we do not have the imagination to let him be useful. Instead we label him "unemployable." We pay him to be useless and heap upon his family an indignity which few of us would be able to bear.

In doing so we invest in human misery.

BLACK AND POOR

On Oct. 25, 1920, Wilma Lee Collins was abandoned in Harlem at the tender age of 15 days.

I got to know her 43 years later on the Lower East Side as Mrs. Wilma Harris, mother of seven children and grandmother of seven more, a woman whose pilgrimage in Harlem illuminates through quiet suffering the plight of the Northern Negro in our rich land.

I

Wilma was born out of wedlock. Two weeks later her mother paid a baby-sitter to take care of Wilma for a day. But her mother never returned. The baby-sitter was Anna Ridge, a girl in her early twenties who lived on West 115th Street in Harlem. Anna Ridge became the only mother Wilma ever knew, even though she never legally adopted Wilma.

Shortly after Wilma arrived, Anna Ridge and her husband took jobs as cooks for a wealthy man who had a large estate on Long Island. Wilma remembers living in his mansion and playing with children who lived nearby. When Wilma was about four years old Mr. Ridge died on Welfare Island of a heart disease, and Mrs. Ridge moved back to Harlem, where she became superintendent of an old tenement building in 131st Street.

Being "super" of a building is a man's job, and it doesn't pay much, but it did give the two of them a free apartment and a few dollars to live on. Mrs. Ridge had to carry out garbage and ashes, shovel coal, clean the furnace, and keep the building in order. This was especially difficult for her because she was heavy and her health was not good. She also baked and sold bread to make ends meet.

"My mother [Mrs. Ridge] was very religious," Wilma explained. "She was a Baptist. She had a hard life, but she never got angry or would try to get even with people. Before I started school she got married again. My father was a good man but not a Christian. He just didn't believe. He was good to me and my mother. He drank

but was never abusive. I don't remember what kind of work
my father did until the Depression came and he went to work for the
WPA at Bear Mountain [now a state park 30 miles north of the
city]. He took us up there a few times. It was wonderful."

Wilma liked going to school and did well. In Harlem, although
the children were all Negro, most of her teachers were white.
Wilma had only four Negro teachers, none in junior high or high
school.

"The schools weren't overcrowded then. Teachers helped us
individually. Sometimes they would even come to the pupils'
homes to visit, but not now. Now the teachers send notes home and
the kids can fool everybody. We had about 15 or so in a class, but
now they have twice as many, and the teacher can't pay as much
attention. They try hard, but the problems are too big. Today the
schools are too crowded, and the teachers can't control the kids."

"I had clothes given to me at school, like most of the kids.
The teacher would give out clothes as she noticed the need. They
were always new — and all made the same. Girls' shoes were the
same as boys'. That was in grade school. In high school we had to
have a skirt and a blouse. I never had more than one skirt and two
blouses, so lots of times I had to wash at night what I wore the
next day.

"We got free lunches in school — hot lunches at noon, and most of
us also got breakfast by coming 15 minutes early to school for
jellybread sandwiches and hot chocolate."

The one event that stands out from her school days is having
both legs broken when a car struck her.

"I was about twelve at the time. The man who hit me didn't have
any insurance, but on paydays he would bring in candy or fruit and
give my mother a little money. That was the first time I really
heard how my mother got me. The social worker sent me out of the
room to talk to my mother about it, and I overheard them.

"The only real fun I had in my youth was the Christmas after
I broke my leg, because I got lots of toys and clothes. That's the
only time it ever happened. The man who hit me and the social
worker brought me lots of things.

"Otherwise life was very hard for me and for my mother.

I used to work like the devil after school. I did all the housework and shopping. Then I helped the man who sold vegetables on
a stand, and for that I got some vegetables late Friday for the
weekend, plus a few dollars now and then. Lots of kids did that.
Before that — before I was a teen-ager — I used to sell shopping
bags, two for three cents. We bought them for a penny apiece.
You could make $2 some Saturdays.

"When I was about 17 years old my father died. He was in his
late thirties. He was sick at home. One day he fell and hit his
head on a corner of the coal stove and died four hours later.

"After my father's death my mother went into partnership with
a friend of hers who was a crippled veteran. The veteran's bonus
came through, and he put up the money to open a little restaurant,
and she did the work. But it was open just a few months. Then
my mother got sick. It was her first stroke. The work was too hard for
her. She had to work from five in the evening till three in the
morning, and she had a bad heart. She weighed 280 pounds. She
never got well."

A few months after her father's death, Wilma graduated from
a Harlem high school and got a job working in a laundry and
doing housework. She was trained as a secretary but it wasn't
possible to get secretarial work. Even some who graduated with
honors could not. This was in part because of the Depression, but
often it was because of color.

"I remember some girls who were hired by doctors to do
secretarial work *and* domestic work, but they were paid as
domestics. And when references were given for other jobs, it was
always as maids or housekeepers. Even with housework the ads
would sometimes put in 'white,' and sometimes if it didn't say, the
position would suddenly be filled — and you never knew. Once
I got a job as a nurse's aid at Harlem Hospital. I took some
courses and worked for two months, but was laid off to make room
for a refugee who was sponsored by a friend of the boss. You never
know whether it's prejudice or not."

When Wilma was 18 years old she gave birth to Kathleen, and
afterward married Kathleen's father, William Harris, 22, who
worked as a clerk in a 5-and-10 variety store. Since Wilma's father

had died the previous year, her ailing mother shared with them
a ground-floor apartment on Eight Avenue near 145th Street. It was
a 3-room, cold-water flat with a coal stove for the winter and
a small gas stove for summer cooking. It rented for $18 a month.

Three months after their wedding William was arrested for break-
ing into a hardware store and was sent to prison on Rikers Island in
the East River. Wilma found out later that he had a compulsion for
stealing which had gotten him into trouble as a child.

"William would be good for a while, and then he would get into
trouble again. When he was home he was a good provider and
good to the children. He was a machinist, and he never had
trouble getting jobs. He worked in garages and in a printshop and
did electrical work. The first time he was in jail for three months.
Then he was sent away for 18 months to a state prison at Elmira.

"The first time he was taken away it didn't bother me too much.
I thought he would be back again and everything would be all
right. I could visit him every day at Rikers Island. Besides, I saw
a lot of this going on in Harlem — broken homes and suffering — and
maybe that's why I wasn't so upset."

The three of them — Wilma Harris, her partly paralyzed mother,
and her infant daughter were on relief. They got $13.80 twice
a month for everything, including rent. Paying $18 a month rent left
less than $10 a month for all three to live on, an impossibility.
So even though it was illegal, Wilma Harris did what people on
relief were expected to do — make whatever money she could on the
side. She did so by working two or three days a week as a domestic.
And she stood in line for bread.

"The bread was in the middle of the block on 124th Street. The
lines were long, sometimes a block long. One line would go to
Seventh Avenue and another to Eighth Avenue. It took a long
time because the same line would have people who wanted meals
and those who wanted bread. I went once a week regularly for
a year or two for bread. The bag of rolls was just about enough to
last a week. Later on at the food depot they gave me things like
oatmeal and canned milk. Once in a while we got sugar, but you
never knew ahead of time.

"They also had depots for sheets and clothes. The investigator would write on a slip what you needed. Then they started the policy of giving you money direct. Sometime during the forties I can remember getting $25 every two weeks and paying $28 a month for rent. So I still had to work. We were living around the corner on 144th Street then. The lady downstairs was in the same position, so we took turns working and taking care of the kids."

The family was fatherless in all but name.

"William spent most of his time in prison. He was home a year after the first time, but after that he was back only long enough to start another baby, and then he'd get in trouble again. Always for stealing, and he always got caught."

Babies have a way of ignoring prison sentences, and so they arrived: Kathleen on May 30, 1938; Edward on Nov. 19, 1939; Russell on Dec. 1, 1941; William on Nov. 10, 1943.

In 1941, while Wilma Harris was pregnant with Russell, her mother died of a third and fatal stroke. The next year Wilma moved with her three children to an apartment on West 114th Street, which rented for $28 a month. There she gave birth to William.

In 1944 the family moved to the Bronx for one year, but returned again to Harlem to live in an apartment that was to be their home for the next 16 years. It was on Seventh Avenue near 132d Street, a 7-room flat on the fourth floor that cost them initially $45 a month rent.

After William Harris was sent upstate early in 1943, he was never seen by the family again. His parole officer and a marriage counselor advised Wilma to divorce him. She would have done so, except for two things: First, legal proceedings are costly, and she didn't have the money. Second, the only legal ground for divorce in New York is adultery, and that is exceedingly difficult to prove. In addition, Wilma Harris didn't know where her husband was after he left prison.

As a result, when she married Thomas Cory in October of 1946, she did so without benefit of a legal divorce. She met Cory at a hotel in midtown Manhattan, where they both were working as domestics. On Feb. 7, 1945, Thomas was born to them. Late the next year they married. It was not a happy marriage.

"Cory was nice but crazy jealous. If I went to a union meeting,

Cory would tag along behind and watch from across the street, and then ask me all sorts of questions afterward. It got to be too much. He didn't support well either. We was on welfare part of the time. He was supposed to support Thomas and Angela [who was born Feb. 9, 1951], and welfare the other four. Welfare sent $50.25 twice a month, but that didn't go anywhere. Cory spent money on cars, old pieces of junk that he liked to drive. He always wanted to invent things like a cure for cancer or a cure for colds, so he spent money on that. But he never provided well. He and the children didn't get along."

They separated once for several months and then tried a reconciliation, but in 1959 they were permanently separated.

Support was off and on those years. So was welfare. And so was work for Wilma. For the most part she had to work, because Cory's support and welfare together did not total a living wage. So after Angela was born Wilma got a job in the hotel where she had previously worked. She earned $36.20 a week, minus withholding tax, as a supplement to welfare aid.

All this was complicated in 1953 by Kathleen, her oldest child.

"Kathy was the smart one in the family. She got mostly A's in school, but she had to drop out of the 10th grade because she got pregnant with Ronald. She was only 15 then. Kathy was scared. She was trembling and wouldn't say a thing, but I could tell. She admitted it when I said we would go to the doctor and see."

In 1955 welfare discovered that Wilma had been holding down a job without notifying them and while drawing welfare assistance.

"I was fingerprinted. They took me to court. I felt terrible. I got sick and cried for days. The case was postponed five times before a judge finally heard it. He called me a fraud. But I told him I was trying to support my family the only way I knew how. I couldn't depend on Cory."

Wilma was required to pay welfare $30 a month. She did so for six months, but couldn't keep it up, so welfare reduced the bill to $20 a month, and a year later to $10. (In March of 1965 welfare told her she had paid over $1,500, but still owed $1,600, which she is now permitted to repay at the rate of $5 monthly.)

Meanwhile Kathleen finished high school after she had Ronald and Julia, and got a job as a dietician's assistant at St. Vincent's Hospital in 1957, earning $45 a week. Kathleen had to drop the job when her mother became ill with pneumonia, but resumed work at a hospital in the Bronx until her third child, Donald, was about to be born. That was in 1958. In 1959, when Kathleen began carrying Raymond, Wilma took out $250 from a loan company to help them out, a loan she was to pay back at the rate of $13.66 a month for two years. However, Wilma herself became pregnant with Karen the next year, and so her work and the payments on the loan were interrupted until she could begin work again — although the interest mounted.

Karen was born June 1, 1961, about the time Wilma Harris (the name she used again after separating from Cory) fulfilled a long inward groaning and moved out of Harlem.

Her daughter Kathleen made the first move. For a Negro on welfare to find an apartment outside the ghetto is not easy, but Kathleen found one on East Sixth Street in the Lower East Side in a building that included many families on welfare. She moved with her (now) five children into a 2-room apartment — two shabby rooms that cost $100 a month rent. Months later Wilma Harris got a 2-room apartment in the same building for $90.

II

When I met them, Wilma Harris and her daughter Kathleen and their children were living on East Sixth Street in a building that dramatizes the cruelty and cost of prejudice. Though it is old and dilapidated and its apartments are tiny (20 of them in this narrow, 5-story building), the rents range from $90 to $115 a month.

Lots of people are paying for an arrangement like that. First of all, the tenants themselves have to pay, psychologically and emotionally, because they find little or no alternative to such living accommodations. Their children pay because they grow up in an atmosphere of noise and disorder, with enormous obstacles against them. Tenants like Mrs. Harris, who are earning their own livelihood, pay outrageous rents. Mrs. Harris now makes $54.20 a week, which is hard enough for anyone to live on in New York City; but on East Sixth Street almost 40 percent of her income goes into rent. The schools pay for such an arrangement in disturbed children. The public pays for it in subsidizing inflated rents for families on welfare. And even more, the public pays for it by investing in a cycle of misery that gathers momentum with each subsequent generation and produces a chain reaction of costs in delinquency, unemployment, and despair. Yet the public keeps on paying to support this cycle rather than pay to break it.

Many profit from such an arrangement too. The landlord does most directly. But so do the banks, who have money tied up in such real estate, and indirectly so do a majority of white Americans who, in one way or another, perhaps through private savings accounts in those banks or through the investments of groups which they support (such as churches or universities) or by their silence, inadvertently support this kind of system.

After living on Sixth Street for two years, Kathleen married and moved to Brooklyn. For the first time her five children got a father. He is Thomas Owens, a towering man who does custodial work in one of the public schools for $90 a week. ("I have a mean boss, but I just 'yes' 'im all the time!")

Mrs. Harris still works at the hotel, and in a way life is more composed for her than it has perhaps ever been, but she has crammed a lot of suffering into her 43 years and has learned to take the ups and downs of life in stride.

"People don't understand what it means to go hungry and to skimp and save to eat and have clothes. Even people who grew up poor forget. They *want* to forget. I've gotten paid on Friday, and Saturday, after buying food, there's nothing left but tokens. Then you have to find someone to borrow from.

"The hardest thing is trying to make things stretch. How to feed a family on a dollar—and then worrying about tomorrow. Who can I borrow from until the next check comes? Then you try to get a few side jobs or take in ironing to make a little money and pay them back.

"It is *not* easy to get on welfare. Welfare says you've got to go to relatives when the unemployment checks run out, even if you have kids. And sometimes the relatives just can't support you. When Kathy was having Donnie, she had to quit work and go on welfare. They tried to make her live with Cory, and Cory just couldn't support them. But welfare was slow in getting through, so Kathy got a dispossess, and welfare won't pay the back rent. She had to get a different apartment. Donnie was born a little early, the evening of the day the first check arrived from welfare. He was born at home that night. Then the doctor came and had them taken to the hospital. The worry and running around did it.

"When you go to welfare, they have pictures on the wall, 'Each child must have three glasses of milk a day!' and signs like that about vitamins and fruits. But what they give you wouldn't allow you to give each child that in a day—or even in a week!

"The investigators [caseworkers] were always nice to me. They were never mean. The one I had when they found out I was working said he knew I couldn't make it on welfare money, but there was nothing he could do. That's the worst thing about welfare. The way it is now, they're making people cheat so they can live right. The way I grew up, that was the only way we could stay alive. There ought to be a way for people on welfare to improve themselves without having to cheat."

Mrs. Harris lived close to lots of unwed mothers on welfare. I asked her how most of them felt about it.

"Most people want to get off. Some won't get off until they are thrown off, but not too many. Maybe 10 percent. The rest would like to be through with welfare.

"It's a big problem with the men. If they have any kind of job at all and marry, they are automatically off welfare. But lots of them don't have steady jobs, like Mr. Prescott. He's a garment worker, so his work is on and off, and if he gets married, he can't really support the family. So they pay two rents and he helps out. It would be lots better for them and for welfare if they got married and welfare would still help them out a little. But the way it is now they can do better not getting married. It's bad if you know that marrying would be making it hard for the family to live. But this way is bad for the kids.

"And the women—some have the feeling that if they get married they're stuck. Maybe he helps out with money now, but if they get married he may lose his job, or maybe he only works part time. And some are worried that after marriage he turns out bad, and she

welfare encourages immorality, dishonesty

can't put him out of the house if they're married. But the biggest worry is money. Most of them would get married if it wouldn't be for that."

The system of poverty and prejudice combine to allow many Negro men to become biological fathers, but not fathers in fact. The price for supporting such a system is fantastically high—morally, emotionally, economically.

Mrs. Harris expresses herself freely about relations between Negroes and whites:

"I played with white children when I was a little girl. That's *all* I played with at first, when my mother worked for Mr. Blake. There were no Negro children. So I never felt out of place with anybody. If I had lived in Harlem all the time it would be different. You have to experience something like that to know it. If everywhere it was mixed, there wouldn't be all this prejudice. You get sick just alike. You can see that what hurts the Negro will hurt the white man too. The trouble is everybody believes the tales they hear, and so both sides think wrong."

What does she think about the South?

"I didn't like it. I spent some time in a little town in South Carolina while my mother was in the hospital. I was about nine or ten years old. My mother's cousin kept me. The colored were not allowed in the theater after five, so we were there from three to five and then we had to leave. And even then they made us sit in the balcony. After eight we had to stay on our side of the tracks. The Negroes all lived on one side of the tracks and the whites on the other.

"But we had more to eat there. Everybody had gardens. I liked the space—but not so much I would want to live there. That was the first time I ever saw a pig or a cow, and I was pretty excited and scared when I touched them!

"My mother grew up in the South. She only went through the second grade, but she could read and write. Then she grew up in Harlem. I don't know why she came to Harlem. My father—the father I knew—went through the fifth grade in Florida, but then he had to go to work because his father died."

I asked her to tell me about Harlem.

"At the hotel where I work even Negro visitors from out of town ask me about Harlem. They seem to think all New York Negroes live there. They ask if it's safe to visit!

"With me Harlem was all right. It depends on the people you associate with. I never had it bad as far as fighting and all that. If you don't bother them, they don't bother you.

"The housing situation is pretty bad, especially with the rats. People seem to have a harder time in Harlem with the landlord fixing anything. They seem to have the attitude, 'The Negroes aren't anything but pigs, and if I fixed it up, they'd just tear it down again.' I heard one of my landlords say that — she wasn't really the landlord, but the agent. They owned five buildings on Seventh Avenue. One of the tenants got up a petition against the landlord, which almost all the tenants signed. She was mad! The petition asked for painting, electric fixtures, ratholes to be covered, and things like that. Two months later it was fixed. But the city knew about the buildings for a long time and had got many complaints before and didn't do anything.

"Kids growing up in Harlem see a lot more of life sooner in practically every way. Sex, for one. In Harlem things like that are talked about in the streets, in front of the kids. It makes it tough for the kids. It gives them the feeling they know everything, when they don't. It ruins them instead of helping them. Sex, language, and drinking is in front of them. The kids imitate what they hear and see, and get into trouble, especially the boys. It's the crowding that does all this."

What was best about Harlem?

"Nothin' was the best! I didn't like Harlem and I don't despise it. But I'm glad I got away. I wouldn't want to move back. Negroes behave themselves better out of Harlem."

She talked about Kathleen becoming pregnant at fifteen.

"In Harlem it's unusual if kids get through without this kind of trouble. All the kids who hung around with mine were in the same boat. It's worse in Harlem now than it was then. Narcotics was just getting started when my kids were young.

"It's hard to raise kids in Harlem. You can keep kids from doing things, but they learn it somewhere else. It's all around. Everybody is crowded together. I think it would have been easier on the Lower East Side or in Brooklyn."

III

Mrs. Harris breathes more easily about her children now. Karen (4) and Angela (13), the two youngest, are still with her. Three of the four older boys have been employed in the garment industry, but because the pay is low and the work seasonal they are looking for steady positions. Only one finished high school and another is married.

Edward, age 25, the oldest son of Mrs. Harris, works as a doorman in a middle-income housing project for $68 a week take-home pay. He went through Machine and Metal Trades School, where he had a good record. He wants a job working on radio equipment or doing some type of machine repairing, but has not been able to secure that kind of job.

He spoke quietly of what it is like to be a teen-ager in Harlem.

"I was glad to move away — not especially because I wanted to move out of Harlem, but because of the family. We didn't get along with our stepfather. He wanted us all to pay our own way, but I couldn't make enough from odd jobs to suit him.

"The bad thing in Harlem was the cops. I got into a lot of trouble with the cops, not doing anything . . . sometimes playing ball or walking the streets or sitting on the stoop. Lots of times they stopped and searched me. They would search you and if you didn't cooperate, they would hit you with night sticks. I was hit quite a few times, but never taken in. They threatened to, though. There were a lot of junkies [dope addicts] around. They shoved you in the hall to search you, and if you threatened not to cooperate, they would say, 'We'll tell them we got something [dope] out of your pocket!'

"The cops also ignored trouble — card games, fights. People cut each other up sometimes in certain bars, but the cops got paid to stay away. If bars didn't pay them off, they'd go in and rough 'em up inside. As far as I know, they were all getting payoffs. They go in bars when it's quiet, get envelopes, and then don't interfere.

"The numbers racket was common. In a store on 125th Street and Seventh Avenue is the biggest bankers in Harlem — the biggest store in New York, as far as the numbers racket goes. Everybody around there knows it. That shop is well protected. The cops are always around. It's never broken into. Cops from two precincts go in there to get payoffs. Everybody knows about it.

"People of Harlem accept this. They figure if people leave them alone, everything is fine, and why poke your nose into trouble? They have a hard-enough time trying to eat and pay rent, so they don't bother much with politics."

I asked Edward about the narcotics problem.

"It's pretty widespread in Harlem. Maybe three out of five fellows on the block were hooked. But maybe it wasn't that bad all over. Most ot the guys who got hooked were past their teens, in their early twenties.

"I think the employment problem has a lot to do with it. When you're high [on dope] you have no problems. People do it to get away. I know two guys who got married, started families, and were doing okay. Then they lost their jobs and were dispossessed. Pretty soon they were high."

Couldn't they have gone on welfare before being dispossessed?

"Welfare is kinda funny. It takes people who don't need it and turns down lots who do. Sometimes they tell you to wait until you get a dispossess, figuring you can get a job. They did that to me, and then still wouldn't give me anything. If you ask me, welfare doesn't help you. If anything, they make it worse. Those guys hit the bottom before they got any help. Then it was too late.

"One kid was found dead in the basement of our house from an overdose. He was young, about 14. But most were older, maybe because there weren't so many young kids on the block."

I asked him if he thought being a Negro was a handicap in trying to get a job.

"I don't have too much problem with discrimination. I've run into it, but I try not to pay too much mind to it. I know lots of big companies where they hire Negroes as porters or truck drivers, and even in personnel, but most of the departments are closed to them."

Edward would like to have a family and move out. Maybe Long Island. Some place where it's not too crowded.

IV

Kathleen is 26 years old and the mother of five. She is married to Thomas Owens, who has legally adopted the children.

Kathleen was always bright and ambitious. After she had Ronald at the age of 16 she finished high school and worked as a dietician's assistant between pregnancies. When that was no longer possible, she often took occasional work at her mother's hotel in midtown Manhattan to help out.

Kathleen had practically no contact with whites until she started working as a dietician's helper.

"I was surprised. I thought they would be bossy or not want to work with me, but they were friendly. Still I was shy about it. At first I imagined I was being used whenever I was given extra work. I was never certain whether I was being used or helped. It scared me and made me shy. Then a lady I worked under noticed it and began talking to me about it. That helped. The race factor makes you act shy. It doesn't pass. At first you wait and see. You expect all kinds of crazy things might happen."

She has largely negative memories of her youth in Harlem.

"People always hung out in the street. There were always accidents. I hated to go shopping. Always crowds and always noise. Even the preacher shouted. I wanted to get out of Harlem.

"Harlem makes you feel disgusted and let down. You feel this way every day. When you get up you don't care anymore. When I was carrying Ronald I said, 'I don't want to stay here. I don't want to bring him up here.' I couldn't stand the house anymore.

"In Harlem there is too much confusion. People all get to feeling the same. They don't care. They don't try. But most of the people can't move out. They can't afford to. They're trapped there. Some people are there so long that by the time they do get something and can move out, they don't.

"The Lower East Side is bad, but it's better than Harlem. On the Lower East Side, at least people are trying to get on their feet. Things were pretty bad in our house on Sixth Street, but some are willing to help out while others go to school or go somewhere to improve themselves. But in Harlem nobody wants to help.

"You have more opportunity to get in trouble in Harlem because nobody cares. On Sixth Street you could send kids in the street and people would watch. Friends would keep track. But in Harlem nobody cares. So most kids get into trouble.

"We hated the cops. It wasn't so much the brutality. The cops just tried to stay away from trouble. Guys could get into trouble and fight, and the cops would walk the other way. We could sit on the stoop and see anything happen — a woman's purse stolen, somebody mugged, a car broken into — anything. I don't know why. Maybe the cops thought the people weren't worth helping.

"Practically everybody smoked reefers [marijuana]. Eighty percent go through that phase. Drinking is a big thing at a certain age too. The girls in the hallway get together and pass it around.

"Then the guys start with goofballs [barbiturates]. Not so much the girls. It's the tough thing to do. Then comes mainlining [heroin injections]. Some of the mainliners were smart, too, good students. In each building there were guys hooked, just about every guy on our block.

"Sonny was the first one found dead. He was 18 or 19. He died from an overdose. Then others. Some went to the service and broke away, but if they came back to live, they got in with the old crowd again and were hooked. I know only four or five who really broke the habit.

"Owens [her husband] went to 'The Rock' — that's the New York Vocational School where all the tough kids go, the ones who are pushed through junior high. Guys and girls there are really hard. Owen's only way out was to go into the service.

"I was worried about my brother Edward for a while because his crowd always was doing something he couldn't do, and it was beginning to bother him. Then something happened to one of the guys, and Edward broke away. Mother gave the boys materials on dope and talked to them. She tried to show them early what harm it did. They knew the bad side. Most parents sorta gave up and didn't teach them. Mother had been out of Harlem and knew what it could be like. Others didn't know, I guess."

Kathleen said that the activities at the community centers and churches didn't help much. "Teen-agers can go into a place like that and just take over."

"You know how a girl feels when she becomes pregnant and isn't married? The first one you kind of accept. You are very scared at first, but you get over your fear and want to help the child. But the second time is really tough. You begin to shy away from everybody. You know you did wrong, so you shy away from people — even your own family, because you know you are hurting them. You know you are putting a burden on them."

Kathleen asked if she could put some of her feelings down on paper. This is what she wrote:

"When I first found out I was pregnant, I was only 15 years old and in my first year of high school. I couldn't believe it was happening to me. I was ashamed and afraid. It seemed as if everybody could look at me and tell that I was pregnant. I began to get sick every morning on my way to school. I was so worried about how my mother would take it. I didn't know if she would put me away or not. When my mother did find out about it she was very understanding and hurt. When I saw her crying, I just wanted to die so that I could not hurt her anymore. I felt that way for months. I was so ashamed of myself I didn't want to be around other people, and when I had to go to the clinic, I was afraid they would be mean to me. But they were very nice and understanding. That made me feel even worse because I knew I did wrong.

"The life of an unwed mother is not an easy life to live. When a girl is raised in Harlem and reaches a certain age, she is expected to go along with the crowd. The crowd is a group of boys and girls all about the same age. Each boy has a girl friend, and as long as you live in that neighborhood, you will be going steady. This is very bad, because after you and the boy have been going steady a few months and you don't go to bed with him, everyone will laugh at you. No one will talk to you, and in school they will just make life miserable, and eventually you will let him have his way and become one of the crowd again.

"In most cases the girl becomes pregnant. Sometimes the boy and girl get married, but in most cases they are too young. So the girl has her baby and tries to make the best of it.

"Nobody bothers you. People just seem to make the best of it.

That is why it is so easy to get caught again after having had one baby. Other boys will try to go with you just to use you, but you don't know that at the time. You really think he cares for you, and after you see him for a few months he will ask you to marry him, and you say yes. Then he would ask you to be intimate with him, and when you say no, the first thing he will say is, 'You did it before, and have a baby.' So you give in, because you think he will marry you, and you don't want to lose him. But after he has his way with you, you don't hear anything else about marriage, and when you get pregnant you don't see anything of him again, and so you are left with another baby to take care of.

"Then being on welfare is like being boxed in with no place to go. You never have enough money to live on, and men know this. They take you out, give you money — not much, but to a woman on welfare anything extra is a big help, and men know this."

Kathy began talking again. "I was going to marry Donald's father. Then, when I was seven months pregnant, I went to see his mother and found out that he was already married." She was quiet for a moment and seemed to be looking through the wall. "In Harlem, kids get together too quick," she said.

It was a big disappointment to Mrs. Harris when Kathy got pregnant. "I could see all the misery ahead of her, and I was hurt. But I didn't let it get me down," she said. "Life has been pretty good to me, considering I had nothing when I got here. I've had some hardships, but I've seen lots of people who had worse, and they survived."

V

The face of poverty is not the same for the Harris family as it is for the Millers. The Millers are held back by poor health and lack of skills and education. But they have the mobility and acceptance that even impoverished white people enjoy, plus the tradition of strong family ties. The Harris family was deprived of these assets. And so the tragedy of the suffering Mrs. Harris and her family have experienced is that it is a suffering we have imposed upon them as a penalty for being black, suffering that emerged almost inevitably from the condition of the Negro ghetto.

Statistics speak to this with eloquence. Most of our nation's poor families (about 80 percent) are white because most of our people are Caucasian. But look at the percentages within groupings. If you are a white American, your chances of being poor are about one in five. If you are a Puerto Rican American, your chances are one in three. If you are a Negro American, the odds soar, and you have about a 50-50 chance of being swallowed up in poverty. The 1960 census shows that 49 percent of Negro families had incomes below $3,000 a year, and most of these lived in city ghettos. Negroes earn on the average barely half as much as whites, and the disturbing fact is that the percentage gap widened during the decade of the fifties.

There is a high concentration of poverty in the South. About two fifths of the whites who are poor and almost three fourths of the Negroes who are poor live in the South. That statistic alone should suggest how impossible it is to understand poverty in America today, particularly the reason for poverty among Negroes, apart from the institution of slavery. However, the stereotypes which most Americans use betray the fact that they make no attempt to understand the plight of the Negro in America today against the background of slavery. "The Irish and the Germans made it. Why don't they?"

But the Irish and the Germans were not captured and brought to this country in slave ships. Their families were not torn apart. They were not systematically isolated from everyone else who spoke their language. They were not stripped of their history and their culture. They were not bought and sold as cattle. Their wives and daughters were not open game for the lust of their owners or compelled to give birth to children who would have to live under the most wretched conditions, and who perhaps in turn would be separated from their families and sold. Their men were not robbed of their manhood — permitted to have sex but denied the basic human dignity of being real husbands and fathers, a tragedy that still leaves the Negro man a weak family figure. The Irish and Germans were not fed a religion that put them in their place as property. It is no use romanticizing all of this by imagining a group of carefree "darkies" gathered "in the evening by the moonlight."

Not only slavery but post-emancipation slavery was stacked against the Negro in America. Though he was legally freed a century ago, slavery had denuded him of every preparation for freedom. Dirt poor, illiterate, and stripped of ambition, without a healthy family pattern, and indelibly marked by his color, all the odds were against him. His emancipation opened few new doors, or opened them only to slam them shut. Myths were perpetuated about the innate inferiority of blacks and used as a cruel excuse for keeping him back.

In the South extreme measures were taken to compel the Negro to remain as impotent and servile as possible. In the North the situation was better, but there a more subtle and respectable form of racism crowded the Negro into prison-like ghettos, and both isolated him from the rest of society and saw to it that he got only the worst jobs, the worst homes, and the worst schools — the jobs, homes, and schools that nobody else wanted. It became a truism that the Negro is the "last to be hired and the first to be fired."

In all of this, it must be said, the church quietly assented.

It is sheer escapism to dismiss this by saying, "I'm not prejudiced," or "We don't have the problem where I live." We are not hermits. We live in an inter-related society which piously sanctions a system that discriminates. Thus we can reside in a neighborhood whose homes and schools are not open to Negroes, but because it is the "system" that does it, we are graciously excused from having to engage in personal acts of inhumanity, and so we imagine ourselves to be relieved of any blame. We participate in the system, however, and the system discriminates with malicious precision.

That is why the "Northern liberal" has come in for so many critical knocks lately. He lives in the illusion that if his personal feelings toward Negroes seem to be all right, the problem for him is solved. As a result, the Northern liberal has acquired a certain hypocrisy that the Southern racist does not employ. In the South more cards are on the table. This helps to explain why many believe that, in the long run, Negroes in the South may be better off than those in the North. It helps to explain why it is so frustrating to be a Negro in the North, where one is offered more freedom but denied the conditions that can give his freedom flesh and blood.

North and South the Negro is trapped in a vicious cycle of discrimination in employment, housing, and education. Housed in the
ghetto, he pays higher rent for inferior quarters and is isolated from
the rest of us, left to rot in the injustices of many generations. In the
ghetto he will go to the most deficient schools, and lacking a decent
education, he cannot prepare himself for a better job. Because
there aren't enough jobs to go around and wages are low enough to
make people stay poor, the Negro finds himself at the bottom of the
employment heap. And without the earning power of a better job
he cannot escape the ghetto. In this way we have locked the
Negro into poverty.

POSTGRADUATE POVERTY

I

Henry Kohler is tall and slightly stooped at 78, but when
he shuffles his thin frame over the floor, it reveals traces of strength
and flesh now gone. He is a kindly man, with tenderness in his
speech. He lives on East 12th Street, where he was born and has
lived all his life, except for two years in the nation's capital.

"I have never been proud of my life," he says. "Maybe that's
a negative way to look at it. Actors can make a good show of
everything, but I can't do that."

Kohler likes to talk about astrology and health foods — perhaps
because he is a lonely man and in poor health. With poor vision
and a weak heart, he worries about his health and the future.

Kohler's only income is the $40 he gets each month from social
security. Half of that pays the rent on his tiny apartment. He
"lives" on the other $20.

He could go on welfare and almost double his income. The
$33.20 a month more he could get would still represent a state of
poverty, but it would give his standard of living an impressive
boost. But he doesn't want to go on welfare, for welfare would
deal a demoralizing blow to his pride, nor does he like the indignity of having welfare investigators checking into his personal
affairs. Like a host of other elderly Americans, he prefers to eke
out an existence on his own meager pension rather than become
a ward of the state. "I'm not starving," he says.

Henry Kohler was born into poverty. His father came from
Germany at the age of 16, married a girl from the Lower East Side,
and worked as a roofer and plumber, but had no steady work
because he was not well. He died when Henry was about 14.

"Luckily my mother was healthy and a hard worker. She did
housework for a doctor. She was a great church worker. I was very
close to my mother.

"Five boys and four girls were born in our family, but some died
before I was born and some when I was small. Only two sisters and
two brothers survived to adulthood, and I was the youngest. The

brother who was nearest to me in age fell off the roof of a tenement
house playing with pigeons and was killed when I was 14. The
others were quite a bit older. So I look up to older people. They
often know more. My sister Alice was 12 years older than me, and
she took care of me a lot."

"Harold was 7 years older than me, and he became a brick-
layer. Wilfred was 15 years older, and he was like a father to me.
He took the place of my father when he died. Wilfred worked in a
bank, and then he studied law, but he wasn't successful at it until
later years."

Kohler still has lots of memories of the block on 12th Street.
He remembers huge election-day bonfires in the street. Also the teen-
age gangs who used fists, not knives. He remembers the waves of
immigrants that swept over the block, each leaving behind some
traces of their stay.

"The Germans and Irish were on the block when I was young. Then
the Italians started moving in. At first they were upper-cut
Italians, but then we got some Sicilians, a tougher bunch. The
Poles were next, and after World War II the Puerto Ricans came.
Now the block is mostly Puerto Rican, but there are still some from
the old groups — and Village people. The [Greenwich] Village
people and students live here now, and some Negroes."

Henry Kohler's life was largely one of indecision and drift.

"I went through primary school — I even skipped one class — and
went on to high school," he recollects, "but I dropped out after
a year and a half, I liked the out-of-doors, and I lost interest in
studying.

"I used to swim in the East River at the old 18th Street baths. But
I got an infection in my eyes from swimming there, and from then on
my eyes got worse.

"I got some jobs as errand boy for a few dollars a week.
Then a Sunday school teacher at St. Goerge's, an Englishman, took
an interest in me. He used to get boys positions on Wall Street.
He was manager of R. H. Hooper Company Cotton Exchange, so
I started there as an office boy.

"Then I went to a stenography school and gradually became
a clerk, earning about $10 a week. I was maybe 17 then. I hoped

to go south as a cotton buyer eventually, but that never happened.

"I was there 12 years as a clerk and earned about $100 a month. The office was growing, but I didn't get an increase for several years. I grew restless and quit. After that I moved from job to job.

"I saved some money all those years, but I also lost a lot speculating on Wall Street. It was like a sickness. I'd be lucky one day and the next day lose everything. I lost hundreds.

"Then I got a notice from the War Department in Washington offering me a stenographer's position there. That was in 1917, and I was about 30 years old. They rejected me for the draft because of my eyes.

"I was in Washington two years. I could have stayed. They wanted me to handle photos and composite them, but I wasn't interested at the time, so I came back after the war.

"I did part-time work typing. Then I took a fireman's job for a while, but it was dirty work, and inhaling the dust made me sick, so I quit that. One summer I worked as a lifeguard at Rockaway Beach. I liked that, being out of doors. Then in 1920 I worked on the census.

"Up to this time I had saved up some, and during the twenties I could live cheap. But I was like a wanderer. After the war a lot of soldiers came home and sort of had the attitude that they didn't need to work, that the world owed them something. I guess maybe some of that rubbed off onto me. I was living at home still, and I wasn't always so well, and after a while I got to thinking maybe I couldn't work. So I got odd jobs off and on, but never had any steady work.

"I never felt sure of myself. It was that way with marriage too. Once my older sister discouraged me. She made a remark about the big nose this one girl had, and that bothered me. Somehow I never felt ready for marriage.

"After the Depression came, outside jobs were all I could get. Then in 1934 my left eye went dead—a detached retina.

"During World War II I used to go to Coney Island once in a while for cheap rides, and someone said to me, 'Why don't you get a job as a watchman for the ships?' So I did. At first I got $6 a day working weekends, and then entire weeks for about $45 a week. But then, at the end of the war, I was out of a job again, and getting near the age of 60.

"For a while I got $18 to $20 a week unemployment, and when that ran out, my sister gave me $25 a month to carry on. I wouldn't go on relief. Then I started getting my $40 a month social security. My sister paid the electric bill, and on Christmas and on my birthday she would give me a little something. Alice was always close to me. When my mother died in 1939, she said, 'Go to Alice.'

Since 1936 Kohler has been living in his 2-room apartment, which is cluttered with lots of old papers. "Holding on to useless things is a problem for old people," he says philosophically. The apartment is shabby. Sometimes the heat is off during winter days, but he doesn't want to complain. "If I complain, it's for the benefit of all, but I get the blame. They may feel the same way about it, so nobody complains."

He pays $20 a month rent — just about rock bottom in New York — plus $5 for gas and electricity. That leaves him about 50 cents a day to live on.

"I get things from supermarkets. I got acquainted with some of the clerks, and they often give me things that are going to be thrown out at one third the price. I don't eat too well, but then, I don't feel much like eating. It's nicer eating with others. At home you are surrounded by worries and problems."

I asked Kohler what some of the worries and problems of old people are.

"Health — that's the biggest worry. In 1934 I lost my eyesight. My right eye had a detached retina and never recovered from it. I was useless after that. I saw light for a while, and then my eye went completely dead. That worried me. Then I had a hernia. The doctors told me there was no connection, but I think there must have been.

"Old people are afraid of dying. It's hard being old, and some people say they wish it was through, but I don't think that's normal.

"You get tired when you're old, and you aren't able to do things. It takes twice as long. Your reactions are slow. When I'm outside, I can make up my mind to do certain things, but when I'm in my apartment it all vanishes.

"Being alone is a problem. You lose your friends and loved ones. I even felt bad when I lost my cat. I've had pets all my life, and I still miss my cat.

"Living in one place too long gets you down too. 'A new broom sweeps longer' — or something like that. It makes you feel old. I hate to tell my age. People look at you as though you're on the way out.

"The older people seem to do the worrying. They worry more about little things. When I was younger, there was always some-body behind the scene. But now I have to fight the battles myself. I always feel I'm not living right, and somebody's going to intrude.

"Money — that worries people. All my life's been worrying about rents. This poverty stuff now is just a political gimmick, don't you think?

"I think the farm is a much better place to live than the city — but poverty is just as bad on the farm as in the city. But then, on the farm they always have plenty of food. They can grow their own, and it's natural food, straight from the soil.

"If I was living as nice as you are, I might be arrogant. I might become inflammatory and overdo myself. My opinions might come out too much in the open. I work better behind the scenes. Maybe being poor has been good for me."

"As nice as your are" — I thought of the modest setting of our almost ancient parish house, a small, crowded building with cracking plaster and soot-gray curtains and then remembered that it represented a style of life far beyond the reach of Kohler and millions of other elderly Americans.

II

Margaret Hemmingson is a wiry wisp of a woman. She has seen 81 years go by — and now she can count more years than pounds. Mrs. Hemmingson's sole source of income is the $86 monthly check from social security.

"It's not quite enough," she observes.

Out of her social security check $40 goes for rent, and the rest goes for food, clothes, gas, electricity, and "incidentals." She has a modest savings in the bank, but that is being rapidly eaten up by hospital expenses. The dwindling of her savings in turn has jeopardized her chances of getting into a nursing home.

Mrs. Hemmingson has been conditioned by a life of hard knocks to face her declining years bravely, but she admits it isn't easy. She worries a lot now.

She was born in Hamburg, Germany, in 1883. Her mother died while giving birth to her, so she and a 2-year-old sister were put into a girls' home. There they grew up.

Her father worked as a longshoreman in Hamburg, and by the time Margaret was 16 he had saved up enough money to send his two daughters to the States. Some years later he also emigrated to this country.

The two girls stayed with an uncle in Hoboken, New Jersey, until they got jobs as domestics, earning $2 a month in addition to room and board. When Margaret reached the age of 20, she married a young truck driver, who delivered seltzer water to grocery stores. The two of them lived in an apartment on East 64th Street in Manhattan, near First Avenue. That was in 1903.

In 1905 Margaret gave birth to Lester. When he was three and a half years old, he caught diphtheria. Four days later Lester died.

Joy and sorrow struck again in short order. Two years after Lester's death Margaret gave birth to another boy, Freddy. "I begged God, 'Oh, please give me my Lester back again!' and He did. But when Freddy was three years old my husband died of pneumonia."

Margaret was a widow at 30.

"I went back to housework again. What else could I do? I worked for 75 cents a day — but we were paying only $10 a month rent. Sometimes the neighbors took care of my baby. Sometimes I would take him along with me when I did housework because he was a good boy. I never had any trouble with him."

For about 15 years Margaret worked as a housekeeper helping her son Freddy through grammar school and seeing him get started first as a delivery boy, then on a cleaning job in the railroad yard.

In November 1929, at the age of 45, Margaret became Mrs. Hemmingson. Mr. Hemmingson worked for the sanitation department and was 10 years younger than Margaret.

"He wanted a good housekeeper, and he saw how good I could keep house. I went through the change of life and was cranky and sickly sometimes, but he put up with it. We got along well together. He liked to travel and see things. Once we went down to Florida in 1940 with my son and his family."

For a year Mr. and Mrs. Hemmingson lived in the Washington Heights section of Manhattan; then they moved to East Fifth Street on the Lower East Side.

"My father was living on this same block. He was an old man and had a stroke, so we moved down to be near him. We rented this apartment for $18. When we moved into the neighborhood my daughter-in-law said, 'Why do you want to live in the slums?' I told her, 'The slums are good enough for me.' We had nice rooms. We had friends and liked it here."

Mrs. Hemmingson's 4-room apartment has been her home for about 35 years. Not many apartments on the Lower East Side are in such good shape. The building is old, but the landlord lives in the building and keeps it remarkably clean. There are no children in the building, so it is a quiet place to live, and a quiet apartment on the Lower East Side is a rare commodity. Her current rent of $40 a month is a bargain.

Mrs. Hemmingson never knew how much her husband made. "He always gave me an allowance each week for household expenses, and from that I was usually able to put away a few dollars into my savings account."

In 1956 Mr. Hemmingson quit work because of a bad heart. Fifteen years earlier he had switched from the sanitation truck to a job as a watchman on the Hudson River docks because he couldn't lift garbage cans anymore. In 1956 he was home, and sick. Though Mrs. Hemmingson was 72, she got jobs again doing housework.

"I earned a dollar an hour, but three or four hours a day was all I could do. It wore me out and I was exhausted. At first it wasn't so bad because my husband got unemployment checks, but after 26 weeks that stopped. Then we started living off social security. But there were doctor bills, and for a while we just couldn't pay for everything. We couldn't pay the gas and the electricity bill, so it was shut off. I used to sneak downstairs and heat soup in the basement. They had a big coal stove in the basement for hot water, and sometimes I took care of it, so the landlord said, 'Sure, any time you want to use the stove, you go right ahead.'

"My son wanted to pay, but I wouldn't let him. 'You have your problems and your family to worry about, and we want to take care of this ourselves,' I told him. Then in three months we got about $150 back on income tax, so we paid the bill. No light at night. We didn't eat proper. That was the hardest point in my married life."

On Good Friday of 1958 Mrs. Hemmingson found her husband dead in bed.

"His union left me $1,500, and we had $500 funeral insurance. The funeral cost $800. I made it as simple as I could. The rest I put in savings.

"Eleven months later my Freddy died."

After her husband's death Mrs. Hemmingson pulled her bony little 74-year-old frame together and began working harder than ever.

"Sometimes I made $15 a week, sometimes $20 or $22. I worked for four different ladies. Sometimes I was tired and just couldn't make it."

Mrs. Hemmingson got along well under the circumstances. Her income was her meager earnings plus the $86 she drew each month from social security. But doctor bills began to mount. Her biggest problem was dizzy spells, caused by slowly hardening arteries. Occasionally she would black out.

Mrs. Hemmingson's condition was aggravated in 1963 when she was assaulted in the hallway of her building by a man who grabbed her by the throat and stole her purse. He was probably a junkie, an addict who, like all addicts, had to steal to finance his habit. He left her unconscious for a short while, but, even worse, he left her terrorized. Mrs. Hemmingson still bears a lump on her throat from that encounter. After that she had to "doctor" even more.

Still she kept on working as much as she could. But the dizzy spells got worse and she blacked out more frequently.

"But I have good neighbors, wonderful neighbors. The people

upstairs and downstairs, and the Riedels across the hall. They help me anytime I need help, but I don't like to bother them. Mrs. Riedel called the doctor for me one night. And once I collapsed on the bathroom floor at three in the morning and I couldn't get up. I knocked on the pipe, and in two minutes the man from upstairs came down to help me.

"Then the night Clara from the church and her husband were here, and they were afraid I was going to die. Clara called the doctor, but the maid answered and said, 'The doctor is not in.' Clara called the ambulance, and we waited and waited, but the ambulance didn't come, so finally they called the police, and the police took me to Bellevue [Hospital]. I didn't really want to go. They were more excited than I was."

Mrs. Hemmingson's 43 days at the hospital proved to be a costly source of worry for her later. Bellevue is an antiquated, crowded city hospital. Mrs. Hemmingson was in a large ward with 30 or 40 other patients, not the finest of surroundings, although she had nothing but kind words to say about the care she received.

Six weeks after she left the hospital she got a bill for $1,935. It had cost her $45 a day.

"Now I won't be able to get into the nursing home," she worried. "I promised them my whole savings, $6,000."

I phoned Bellevue Hospital. I phoned the Department of Hospitals, Division of Collections, which issued her bill. I went to the hospital and spoke to administrators, then to the collections office. I begged. I pleaded. I got sore. Always the story was the same. The most anyone over 65 is allowed to have in private savings is $950, or they cannot consider reducing the bill. "Her case is not unusual," they said.

"If I can't get into my nursing home in Jersey," says Mrs. Hemmingson, "then I'm going to stay right here and make the best of it. My doctor says I shouldn't be alone, but I have good neighbors. I'll get by."

I talked to her doctor. He said there was no need for her to be in the hospital so long. "It's blood money," he said, when I told him of the bill.

What is her biggest worry? "When I get sick is the biggest worry.

Bills keep coming in just the same. If only I could work!" she says
with a sigh.

"I don't know where I would be if I didn't get social security.
Medicine is so expensive. It costs me $3.50 a bottle, and if I have
to call the doctor, it's $10. It used to be $5, but now it's $10.

"I waited until I was 72 to take social security. I know lots of
old ladies who get $40 or $50 a month. How do they live? How do
they make it?

"Being alone is hard too, but I'm not crying about it. I always
try to keep a sense of humor. I do the best I can. The Lord has
been good to me. I just wish He would take me away. What good
am I to anybody? But I have no complaint. I have everything
I want—if I can only get in the home."

Mrs. Hemmingson has memories. She has a picture of 3-year-old
Freddy sitting on her lap when she was 29 and a strikingly attractive
lady. She has pictures of the family's trip to Florida in 1940. But
she doesn't look at these often because she doesn't like to live in
the past. And when she thinks about the future she worries.
She gets $86 a month. The rent is $40. Medicine is $14. Mrs. Hem-
mingson squeaks by somehow on the remaining $32.

III

Halfway down the block from Mrs. Hemmingson, in the same
building on Fifth Street in which her father once had an apartment, lives her brother-in-law, Harry Elliott, a smiling, vigorous,
white-headed man of 86.

Mr. Elliott pays $24.15 for two dismal, barren rooms that offer an
immediate contrast to Mrs. Hemmingson's apartment. The furniture
consists of a few old, drab pieces—a bed, a kitchen table, a chest
of drawers, and a chair for each room, plus the tub in the kitchen.
The tub has a lid, so like most bathtubs on the Lower East Side
it doubles as a place on which to pile things. The walls are a dirty
gray, and the pattern on the linoleum has long since faded to match
them. The walls are bare except for an old wedding picture and
a picture of his father-in-law—both oval-shaped photos—and a
calendar on the closet door, all in the kitchen. The closet is only
12 inches deep, so Mr. Elliott hangs a few things on a small rope
strung across a corner of his bedroom.

The room is heated by a small gas stove which doesn't always work. Several times when I was there in the winter, I shivered next to the cold stove, as Mr. Elliott and I talked across the kitchen table.

Mr. Elliott moved to this apartment in 1963 after his wife died, in order to be near Mrs. Hemmingson. He has no closer relatives. But the neighborhood is strange to him and in some ways threatening. The biggest thing in his favor is his health.

Mr. Elliott was born in Southampton, England, in 1879. Six weeks later his parents came to the United States. Harry grew up on Bank Street in lower Manhattan. His father worked first as a shipping clerk and then got a job in a soap factory on the West Side.

"It was the oldest soap house in America—the Manhattan Soap Company on 36th Street. My father worked there until he was an old man, and then the Depression came and the factory sold out.

"I went to school a few years—no more than four. I was a self-made man! When I was 14 I went to work in the soap factory. I worked there 10 hours a day, 6 days a week, for $3 to $4 a week, and I worked in soap factories for 63 years until I was 77.

"I ran the soap dryer. I drew soap from a big tank, put it on steel rollers, where the soap is chilled. Once the tank above me boiled over and the stuff came through the floor. The lye fell on my back and burned the skin right off. I was out of work for six weeks. That was the only time in my life I ever had to see a doctor—and look at me. I'm 86!"

Mr. Elliott married Mrs. Hemmingson's sister-in-law.

"She was easygoing and never spoke very much. She was very frail but jealous and a little spoiled. Some people say I spoiled her too much, but if we passed a candy store and she complained, I went in and said, 'Give this lady the best box of candy in the house.' She liked to stay at home."

There were no children.

When Mr. Elliott was 47, the soap factory went bankrupt and sold out to a company in Bristol, Pennsylvania, so for seven years the Elliotts lived in Bristol. Then, during the Depression, he was laid off, and for three months he hunted for work. He found it at the John T. Stanley Company on 30th Street, near the Hudson River, where he began work for $14 a week. After 19 years with Stanley he retired in 1956 at the age of 77.

"The most I ever earned was $50 to $60 a week, but it wasn't steady. Sometimes we didn't work a full week when business was off. I think the most I ever made was $1.15 an hour.

"When I retired we bought a summer bungalow on Staten Island. We paid $5,500 for it and had it winterized, but it was too much to pay. Taxes were too high. I was there for six years, until my wife died. Then after she died I sold the house and came over to the East Side to be with Margaret [Mrs. Hemmingson]. She was all alone, and so was I. But I got only $3,500 for the house.

"Now I get $94 a month social security, and I still get $58 a month from the mortgage. I've been able to put $3,000 in the bank so far. The rent is cheap here, but I can't stay. It's a terrible place. I've been robbed three times. They took my gold watch, a garnet ring, my rent money, an overcoat, and a radio. Now there's nothing much they can take, but it ain't safe here. If Margaret moved away, I wouldn't stay here. If my people could see me here right now they'd be amazed. They'd say, 'You're a fool!' They don't know what it's like here."

How does life look to him, and what about the future?

"I'm 86, but I don't look it and I don't feel it! I don't want to go to a nursing home. As long as I can crawl around, I don't want to go to a nursing home. But what if something happened to me?

"Relatives don't care for you when you're old. You're always in the way. You get nice letters and they say, 'Take it easy,' and all that stuff, but they don't really want you to come and see them. I don't have any close relatives anyway, and they're a long ways away, so I don't visit them and they never visit me. Do you think they'd want to come to a place like this? They have their children and their problems.

"Mrs. Hemmingson is different. She's one good, thoughtful little woman. She's done more for me than all my relatives. She got the funeral for my wife and helped me get a place here. She's one good little soul.

"The biggest problem is being lonesome. Margaret says, 'Make friends! Make friends!' But where am I going to make friends? My cousin in California offered to let me live with them, but I know how they treated their father. They say the old fool doesn't know what he's talking about, but the old fool's still got a few brains!

"I'd like to have something to do. I don't like this idleness. I'd rather be working. I'd work, but I don't know where to go, so I just wander around. But where do you make friends? Around here people speak Polish.

"I don't cook for myself. I just make coffee, and sometimes warm milk before I go to bed. That's supposed to help you sleep. I don't sleep as well now as I used to when I was working. Sometimes I get oatmeal, but I don't bother with cooking. Margaret lets me eat supper with her, and I pay her for my meals, but what'll I do if she gets into a nursing home? I'll have to find a furnished room somewhere and eat out, and I can't afford too much."

Mr. Elliott is proud of his sturdy, 86-year-old frame. He smiles and laughs easily, and he talks with compulsive speed. But under the surface of his happy disposition the anxiety of age and poverty gnaws away.

IV

Millions of Americans not only go through the school of poverty during their vigorous years but find themselves enrolled, against their will, in a postgraduate program. The problems of uselessness and loneliness and ill health that commonly haunt the aged are compounded by a struggle for bare existence and the fear that some unannounced setback may topple that precarious balance which enables them to live somewhere on the thin line between security and starvation.

Old people find themselves caught between two opposing forces. On the one hand, their lives have been prolonged, thanks to medical advances. On the other hand, ours is a society which venerates the young and increasingly discards the aged from any meaningful involvement in work or family life. The euphemisms we have developed to gloss over these cruel facts—"senior citizens," "golden agers"—cannot hide the truth that we have learned how to make people live longer without having learned how to let them spend those extra years usefully. For many old people those years are more like slow death than extended life.

The problems of the aged are not caused primarily by poverty.

On the contrary, a good case can be made to show that our nation's wealth is to a great extent responsible for the problems of the aged. That is the irony. In making the widespread enjoyment of medical advances possible, our wealth has produced millions of old poor people.

The problems of the aged poor will not be solved the day poverty is wiped out in this country. Indeed, those problems may then be far more massive. Nevertheless the fact remains that poverty is a heavy burden for old shoulders to bear. Becoming helpless in old age is no fun under any circumstances, but to be poor when one is old is to be more helpless. To be lonely and old is not easy. But if you are lonely and old and poor, you are apt to be more lonely. Poverty is not only a problem by itself, but especially for old people a problem which intensifies other problems. That is true for two reasons. It is true because poverty is a widely accepted symbol of failure so that it acts as a psychological force in aggravating feelings such as loneliness and uselessness. But it it also true because poverty imposes concrete restrictions on old people. They cannot move around as much or go to the movies or see the doctor as often if they are poor.

The poverty that lies in wait for the young and stalks adults slowly strangles the aged.

Across the street from my church is Tompkins Square Park, probably the most densely utilized park in the city. The primary reason this inadequate park is used so much has less to do with the children who swarm in it than with the old people who sit in it by the hundreds. Many of them are old-country people — Polish and Ukrainians — who speak little English, and on warm days they line the benches of the park like people in a crowded pew. They reflect a strange and fascinating mixture of emotions. Some come for a walk, some to play chess or to visit. Or just to watch. For the most part they are quiet. The lines and shadows and shapes of their faces make you want to guess what complex of experiences have carved them so.

Unfortunately the faces too often betray meaninglessness — faces that stare into the past. You know that many are there because they have nothing else to do, and this is the least miserable way

they know how to pass the time. Most of them worked hard to make
a living when they were young and strong, but now they are the
has-beens, and their present poverty attests to that. Many feel
like old shoes thrown away or put into a closet to be forgotten.

About 19 million Americans, 10 percent of the population, are
65 or older. For a variety of reasons it is difficult to tell how many
of these are poor, but it is clear that close to half of them must be
so designated. In 1960 about half of the husband-wife families in
the nation, the head of which was 65 or over, had incomes of less
than $2,900 annually. Of two-person families headed by someone
aged 65 or older, more than one third (36 percent) had incomes of
less than $2,000 a year. For many, such incomes represent abject
poverty.

Since half of our aged population cannot be listed in the
"family" category because they are widowed, separated, divorced,
or single, their incomes are also important, and with them the picture is even gloomier. (More than two thirds of these, it should be
noted, are women.) One may assume that living with relatives
sharply reduces the need for an independent income. Most nonmarried old people do not live with relatives, however. One
third do. One out of 14 is institutionalized. One out of six is listed
as the head of a family. And half of them live alone or in the homes
of nonrelatives. The State of New York, with the highest number of
nonmarried aged persons (843,000 in 1960), ranks 14th among the
states and the District of Columbia in per capita income received by
these people. Yet 57 percent have annual incomes of less than
$1,000, and the median income for those living alone or with non-
relatives was $1,179 a year, or less than a hundred dollars a month.

Since one's income in old age almost always reflects the type of
employment and the level of income earned previously, the best way
to guarantee poverty in old age is to be poor when younger.
However, it is not only the poor and young who become the poor
and old. The poor and old often had adequate incomes earlier but
were not sufficiently protected for old age. Sometimes they could
not live adequately and still save for retirement, and sometimes an
unexpected illness or some other setback devoured their savings and
ruined carefully made plans.

If people are penalized for being old, Negro Americans pay a double penalty — one for age and one for race. It stands to reason that Negroes, underemployed and underpaid before retirement, have little security on which to depend after retirement. Negroes 65 years old and older average two thirds of the income of whites 65 or over in the case of couples, and three fourths the income of whites in the case of nonmarried persons. Even though by percentages that puts elderly Negroes closer to elderly whites in income than their younger counterparts, that is true only because the income for whites has farther to drop. In 1962 the median income of elderly Negro couples was $1,960 a year, about a thousand dollars less than the median income for elderly white couples. The situation with aged nonmarried Negroes is considerably worse, and that spells double jeopardy, since a shorter life expectancy and a higher rate of broken marriages among Negroes leaves more of them fending for themselves after 65. Even more than among whites, the women predominate in this group, and very few manage to escape poverty in old age.

The problems of our old people are mushrooming. We not only have more old people because of population growth, but purely in terms of percentages there are almost four times as many Americans over the age of 65 as there were a century ago. Yet a much smaller proportion are living with their offspring today. For many old people that reflects a conscious choice. For countless others it means they are lonely and discarded. A parallel situation obtains with regard to employment. Today proportionately fewer old people are working, and in the age of automation that trend is growing.

Poverty makes the problems of our old people more agonizing. It makes the old sicker, less mobile, more frightened of the future. It makes them worry harder and longer about their health and about soaring medical costs. It leaves them feeling more useless and more alone.

The Biblical understanding of man certainly leaves no doubt that there are weightier issues for the aged to confront than the problems of poverty. But that understanding should also save us from the cruelty of giving people added years of life and then prescribing that those years be spent in needless misery.

POVERTY — THE DEAD END

How could today's poor have avoided poverty? With or without his physical disability, could Carl Miller have learned a trade and gotten a steady job with promise of security? Perhaps. If he had done so, in all likelihood someone else would have been out of a job, compelled to travel the road of poverty to its dead end.

To see this it is necessary to look beyond Carl Miller and Wilma Harris and Henry Kohler to the picture in the nation as a whole, and in doing so to take into account also the new situation for today's poor that makes poverty so often a place of no exit.

Nobody knows how many poor people there are in the United States. Estimates range from 30 to 50 million. A complex of factors must be taken into account in making an estimate. However, if we use the one most widely acknowledged standard, then $3,130 is the poverty line for a four-member family, and in all about 9 million families and 30 million people are included. Add to that another 5 million unattached individuals with annual incomes below $1,500 and you have a conservative estimate of 35 million poor people, or just about one out of every five citizens. These figures are all the more appalling when you realize that the *average* income for families under $3,130 is well below that figure. And millions of other Americans who do not qualify as poor under these minimal standards live in serious deprivation.

In America today the gap between incomes of $3,000 and $6,000 a year is more startling than the gap between incomes of $6,000 and $60,000. It doesn't make much difference for the essential commodities of life whether you earn six thousand or sixty thousand dollars a year. You can live in a fine home, drive a car, see a movie when you feel like it, enjoy a wholesome diet, and be considered a success in either case. But if your family has to get by on $3,000 a year, few or none of those options are yours. In addition, you may find yourself living in an overcrowded or dilapidated home; your children are apt to be getting an inferior education; worst of all, you may have to face the demoralizing likelihood that they too will be caught in a cycle of poverty from which there seems to be no escape.

When we compare poverty in the United States with poverty abroad, we see that the poor in our country are far more prosperous. Early in 1964 Chester Bowles reported on a debate that had taken place in the Parliament of India. A member of the opposition party contended that the average income of the bottom half of the Indian population amounted to four cents a day, while an administration spokesman argued that it was at least 10 cents! In India people by the thousands literally starve to death on city streets. It is small comfort, however, to remind a seasonally employed father, stuck with his family in a rundown tenement apartment, that there are millions of Asians worse off than they are. He knows very well he is not in Asia but in a wealthy land with a booming economy and that he and his family are being bypassed.

"The poor never had it so good," it is said, and today in our country poor people are clearly better off in some respects than the poor of a generation ago. Actually their improved position is largely superficial. They may have some modern appliances in the kitchen and more toys for their children, but they do not have as much hope or as much dignity. When people describe how it used to be when they were poor, what impresses me most is not the similarity but the difference between poverty then and today. I am struck not by how bad it used to be but by how bad, by comparison, it is now.

A lady who grew up on the Lower East Side and is now modestly prosperous keeps telling me how poor she once was — more so, she believes, than the poor today. Evidence: the clothes children wear and the lunches they bring to school. "We never had the things they do," she says. What she fails to understand is that the whole mentality of poverty has changed. Her father was a printer, who despite his modest salary had a job that made him a respected wage earner. He had grown up in a European tradition which placed a high value on such things as thrift, industry, obedience, and education; and he was well situated to inculcate these virtues in his children. As he assessed himself in relation to his surroundings (the normal measuring stick), he knew he was doing modestly well,

and he could look forward to his children doing better, which
they did.

The poor today are not in such a favorable position. They are the
ones who were left behind when everyone else advanced. They are
more isolated from the rest of society, because the poor of yesterday, who make up the great middle class of today, promoted
themselves to the suburbs. The poor today have a proportionately
smaller share in the nation's wealth than yesterday's poor enjoyed.
The gross national product can rise $40 billion in one year, but it
makes no difference to them. They still have inadequate jobs or no
jobs at all, and often no reason to hope for a change.

Yesterday poverty was the usual starting point for better things.
Today it is the dead end.

Myths About the Poor

The myths and stereotypes people employ indicate that the poor
have never been so misunderstood. That should not surprise us. For
one thing, they have become a minority group for the first time in
our history, and we misunderstand minorities. In addition, we no
longer live next door to the poor, but in our own class ghettos, and
separation breeds suspicion. Above all, we are impressed with the
increasing wealth of our nation, a wealth in which most have shared,
and we are therefore prone to assume that anyone who really *wants*
to can shake off the restrictions of poverty. Failure to do so, we
instinctively believe, is a mark of moral weakness.

This misunderstanding helps to make poverty a dead end for
people because it prevents us from facing the problem honestly and
working for solutions. Below are some standard expressions of this
misunderstanding.

1. *The poor are lazy. Let them make it the hard way like I did.*
This stance assumes two things. It assumes that "I have made it the
hard way." When this assumption is analyzed, it almost always turns
out to be erroneous or highly exaggerated. We are too ready to
give ourselves the credit when circumstances and opportunities may
have been stacked in our favor. For example, how can we equate
the chances of a white baby with the chances of a Negro baby? The
evidence does not permit it.

It also asserts that those who don't "make it" are lazy. But what

is the evidence? During World War II unemployment became virtually nonexistent because jobs were available. During most of
our history there has been a shortage of labor in the country.
When labor is in demand, few are idle. The lesson of life is that
personal achievement is impossible apart from opportunity. Destroy
or curtail opportunity, and you reduce achievement.

2. *Why don't they go out and get jobs?* There are not enough jobs
to go around. Most unemployed people do hunt for jobs, but the
hunting is often for nonexistent positions, and one cannot be
expected to play this game indefinitely. If you think otherwise, try it
for a few years. Many jobs, because they pay little or are seasonal,
do not furnish a living wage. Naturally the unskilled, the ill-
educated, the aging, and dark-skinned minorities suffer the most
from this.

3. *People on relief have it too good.* Let no one kid you. People
on relief live far below the margin of poverty, and they can't
afford any extras — as a look at an itemized list of necessities for
welfare recipients demonstrates. This is living pared down to the
bone. However, you cannot blame a family on welfare for wanting
to watch television, even if they pay for it in food and clothes,
because it may offer them their one escape from an otherwise dismal
existence. To such a family a TV set is far less expendable than for
most of us who have a wide range of choices in recreation and
entertainment. If occasionally a person on welfare spends money
foolishly — on liquor or perhaps expensive flowers — it reflects a wish
to escape one's fate or an agonizing desire to participate in a bit
of America's abundance, even though it means more suffering in
the end.

4. *Why don't they move out of the slums?* Where can they go? And
how would they find work there? And how could they live until
they do? The trend in jobs is to the city, so people must move to
centers of employment. And when one is poor, he lives where the
rent is cheap. For millions of Americans it means there is no alternative to the slums.

5. *Why don't they at least clean up?* To many, uncleanliness is the
final insult. "Cleanliness is next to godliness," they say (though the
truly godly have never been so preoccupied with cleanliness). But

on the Lower East Side cleanliness is next to impossible; at least
there are formidable obstacles. Being crowded together in small
living units with virtually no closet space is one. Waging war with
soot is another. Inadequate service from the city sanitation department, population density, and emotional torment are others.
However, the idea that poor people are dirty is a stereotype that
does disservice to the majority of them, who do rather well against
impressive odds.

What strikes one about the myths that lie behind such questions
is not only that they block understanding but that they reflect
a fierce self-righteousness. The moral superiority they assume and
the ease with which they presume to expose the faults of the poor
raise the question whether those who make such judgments know the
meaning of grace.

At the same time it is often overlooked that the poor have
strengths and virtues. The poor are not impressed with formalities
or with the kind of sophistication that tends to obscure rather than
reveal persons. They are less apt to be prisoners of pride, more apt
to be open about themselves, about life and its problems. They are
better braced for disappointment, more humble in failure. Death is
no stranger to them, and the poor are often much closer to it, more
honest about it than others. They are in touch with the smell
of the street, the violence and passions of men, the sufferings of
their neighbors. As a result they are often more able than others to
sort out and pay attention to actions that really matter and less apt
to get hung up on things for appearance's sake.

Furthermore, a poor man who *is* dirty and lazy is a sick man, and
we ought to have a double sense of responsibility: not to feed his
sickness by isolating him and putting him on the dole but to help
him get well. Especially we ought to take steps to see that the children of such a man are not locked into the same pattern of hope-
lessness.

A basic blunder in trying to understand the poor is the failure to
take into account the raw material out of which they must shape
their lives. An aspiring junior executive in his corporation was
fired, but for months, while he was unemployed, he got dressed and
left the house in the morning as he always did so that he would

not to have to tell his teen-age children he was unemployed. If humiliation and guilt can do that to a professionally trained man, imagine what it means to a man to face his family month after month, perhaps year after year, with no job and no likelihood of a job or able to look forward at best to the most minimal support for his family. Think of the burden of the man who knows he is probably trapped for good in the slums and will never be able to lift his family out of poverty; who realizes that the very situation he is in is likely to predestine his children to the same.

In this situation a whole pathology of poverty develops which is sicker than anything like it a generation ago. The sense of failure and uselessness it produces may have a whole host of repercussions. It may drive a man to seek an escape in alcohol or to abandon his family. His children are more apt to grow up disturbed, restless, and unable to get along in school. They are more likely to be disillusioned about the future — frustrated when they see the growth of the nation but realize that they are not being equipped to have a productive share in it. They may turn to drink, dope, sex, crime, or any combination of these. A girl may crave affection and want desperately to escape prisonlike conditions — and become the victim of the very thing that perpetuates her imprisonment. She has a lover and gives birth to children, in or out of wedlock, and soon finds herself saddled with incredible responsibilities for which she is not prepared. She becomes old and worn out before her time. It is easy to stand morally aloof and criticize her deficiencies; but where do we get the idea that those of us who are prone to criticize, given the same circumstances, would not be just as apt to get caught in the same web?

We can ignore these agonizing truths rather than acknowledge our responsibility for them, but then we should know we are throwing our weight on the side of making poverty a dead end for people.

Employment

There is no way out of poverty for people unless they make enough money. Therefore the most fundamental step away from the dead end is to provide people with jobs — and jobs that pay adequate wages.

Look at the problem of unemployment. Government figures that place the unemployment rate slightly below 5 percent are deceptive because they do not adequately take into account the partially employed, nor do they include those who are not looking for jobs but would be on the labor market if the jobs were available. Years of discouragement and seemingly unsurmountable obstacles have convinced them that it is nothing but an exercise in humiliation to keep on looking.

What do people do when they are neither working nor receiving unemployment benefits? According to the 1964 report on poverty by the U. S. House of Representatives Committee on Education and Labor, public relief is the last resort for most of them. Many of them dip into meager savings, move to cheaper housing, borrow money, sell possessions, or get help from relatives. Whatever is done, the consequences are usually grim.

Unemployed youth presents a particular crisis. According to the House Committee's report mentioned above, in October 1963 one third of those listed as unemployed workers came from the 16-21 age category, and the number of young people entering the labor market each year is accelerating rapidly. School dropouts suffer most. An estimated 30 percent of the youth entering the labor market during the 1960s will be school dropouts. Negroes who enter the market have twice as much likelihood as whites of not finding jobs. One economist of HARYOU, the antipoverty program in Harlem, estimates that in 1965 there were ten thousand persons between the ages of 16 and 21 in Central Harlem alone who needed help in getting employment. Young people who are pressed to find employment in the cities because of dwindling opportunities on the farm are frequently not equipped to compete for urban jobs and have special difficulties.

During the years 1965-70 approximately three million young people will join the labor market each year, but we know that the positions open to these millions of youths will follow the trends of recent years. Professional and technical jobs requiring college diplomas and advanced degrees make up the fastest-growing section of the market. Technical and semiprofessional jobs requiring education beyond high school constitute the next fastest-

growing section, etc. The report observes that during the last
decade jobs filled by high school graduates rose 30 percent, while
jobs for those with no secondary school education dropped 25 percent. About 10 percent of labor market opportunities are unskilled
jobs today, but by 1970 that percentage will be chopped in half.

These figures say some very clear things about future job opportunities for today's children and the desperation which may face
tomorrow's ill-educated youth. The solution, however, is not quite
as simple as seeing to it that everybody stays in school as long as
possible. We have to realize that for some extra schooling is fruit-
less and unbearable. More revealing, the House Committee report
said that during the past decade our growing economy created six
million additional jobs, but in the same period the labor force
grew by eight million. In other words, we are *losing ground
on the crucial matter of jobs.* The war in Vietnam and the helpful
but surface-scratching efforts of the war on poverty may stem the
tide temporarily. The fact remains, we are in trouble on jobs.

What this situation means should be clear to us. Unless more
drastic steps are taken than we are taking now to create new jobs,
we will be dumping more and more rejects on a social garbage
heap where they will become even sicker, more isolated, more
fearful, more hopeless, and more driven to desperation than
today's poor. Each year we will be handing out increasing billions
to let them exist that way. And by our inaction we will be investing
in precisely those vices which produce a hell on earth for their
victims and destroy the moral fiber of society.

The problem of unemployment appears all the more frightening in
the face of automation, which is moving upon us rapidly. As
machines replace men, jobs will be created on top, but more jobs
will be eliminated on the bottom; and evidence from the past
decade indicates that despite an expanding economy which
creates new jobs the elimination of jobs will prevent us from even
keeping pace with the growing labor market unless something is
done. The steam shovel has replaced the pick and shovel. The automatic factory is with us. And in the future computers will replace
many more "think" jobs. Machines can produce more goods but
cannot distribute them. We must see to that. Machines can do more

work, but they also destroy jobs — more jobs than they create. The answer is not to stamp out or even slow down automation, but to step up the creating of new jobs. It is imperative that we tame machines for human service and not let them become our masters. In doing so we may be compelled to revamp radically many of our current assumptions about work and pay and leisure. And we will certainly have both need and opportunity to prepare increasing numbers of people for human services which machines cannot perform.

Joblessness, however, is not alone in producing poverty. Poor wages also produce it. Despair is generated not only when the job market offers no live option to home relief, but also when the jobs which are available pay wages that lock people in poverty.

The federal minumum wage is $1.25 an hour. A man who works a full 40-hour week at an unskilled job for a minimum wage makes only $50 less deductions, or barely $200 a month. On the Lower East Side more than one quarter of his salary is likely to go into rent. If he has a wife and two children, he cannot possibly spend anywhere near a dollar a day per person for food, or he will have virtually nothing left for clothes, utilities, pencils, bus and subway fare, medicine, furniture, and the like. And all the time he will be unable to lay aside anything for the future, so he must look forward to retiring and dying in poverty.

A minimum wage of $1.25 an hour is a poverty wage for a family man. It is therefore doubly disturbing to realize that in 1964 only 29 million workers were covered by the federal minimum wage law. Some of the rest are covered by state laws, but quite inadequately. Twenty states do not have a minimum wage law at all, and this includes a wealthy, industrial state like Illinois. About twelve million Americans earn less than $1.50 an hour, or under the $3,130-a-year bottom for family earners. Men in this category work as farmers, service workers in hotels, restaurants, and laundries, as porters, lumbermen, factory workers, and the like.

The sum of the matter is this: Unless and until we create enough jobs to go around, and unless and until we see to it that wage earners who support families are not stuck with depression-type wages, we will continue to assure today's poor and millions of today's children that the road ahead for them leads to a dead end.

Housing

The 1960 census revealed that one out of every five dwelling units in our nation was either dilapidated or deteriorating. Almost half of the dwelling units for Negroes were so designated. Many others lacked sanitary facilities. Most of those living in the substandard housing lived in urban slums, and as our nation becomes increasingly urbanized, the slums keep increasing.

The poor pay too much for such housing. They pay because there is a tight market on low-rent housing, and the market is being made tighter by slum clearance, which reduces the number of low-rent units available. Right now nobody, the government included, is seriously in the business of supplying suitable housing for low-income people. The Housing Act of 1949 authorized construction of 810,000 such units, a pittance compared with the need, but many of the authorized units have not yet been built. Since that time the government has given massive assistance to the nonpoor through urban renewal projects and through FHA mortgages for home ownership, but the government has largely ignored the poor.

FHA-backed loans mean extensive government assistance in housing. But during the first half of 1965 only $4/10$ of 1 percent of the single family homes purchased through FHA assistance helped families with incomes under $4,000. In fact, most of the houses built and purchased through the FHA are part of the white suburbias that ring our cities and help to isolate the poor in ghettos. Even the FHA's new experimental program to rehabilitate slum tenements will have the effect of boosting rents and may ultimately force many poor families to move elsewhere.

Slums and Social Insecurity, an eye-opening study by Alvin L. Schorr from the Department of Health, Education, and Welfare, sums up the situation this way: "The Government has chosen not to place funds for housing in the hands of low-income families, and it has chosen not to use public housing as its major vehicle." The housing bill sent by the President to Congress in June 1965 helped to document that conclusion. It asked for 35,000 units of low-income public housing each year for the next four years, an amount insufficient even for the needs of New York City, let alone the entire nation. The government's housing policy is an excellent example of an immensely significant but little-recognized fact: that our welfare state invests itself primarily in the "haves" rather than the "have-nots."

The poor pay more than others for their housing in terms of the slice taken from their salaries. If the family income is $2,000 a year, probably more than 30 percent goes for rent. But if earnings are $10,000 a year, more likely only 15 percent will be paid for rent. For the Negro the percentage will be higher in either case and the housing inferior. In Chicago in 1960 the average rent for whites receiving aid to dependent children was $65 a month. The average for Negro families receiving such aid was $83 a month although they were housed in worse quarters.

The poor pay more in what they get for the dollars they invest. Sometimes the ability to put another $20 a month into housing would bring vastly improved accommodations, but the $20 is not there. So the poor pay for it in crowded quarters, leaking faucets, and ill health. Overcrowding is the most serious penalty because there is a striking relationship between overcrowding and mal-adjustment. The child who is never alone cannot look at life with any perspective; he is swallowed up by it. He sees too much adult greed and weakness too soon, and he is overstimulated sexually. Normal family life and independent growth are made difficult. When this sort of thing happens, eventually everybody pays, not only the poor.

The question of housing is serious because people see themselves partly in the light of their surroundings. A person's dwelling has a lot to do with his self-image. That helps to explain — despite their feelings of entrapment and despair — why tenants of slum neighbor-hoods can still have a strong sense of pride and attachment to their homes (a fact which constantly bewilders city planners), and it suggests that the answer to old housing is not necessarily chopping it down. It also helps to explain the growing difference between the slums of the past and the slums of the present.

Michael Harrington draws a sharp contrast between the ethnic slums of yesterday and the slums of today. In *The Other America* he speaks of "the culture of aspiration" which characterized the ethnic

slum but is absent from the new type. The ethnic slum was considered a starting point, not the end. It was a place where new-
comers had hope, and although the slum then saw its share of evil
and misery, still it was built around a stable family life; it offered
a strong sense of identity; and it consciously prepared people for
a better future. Today the slum tends to be less a point of departure
for better things than a dumping ground for those whom the rest of
society has cast off as rejects. They are rejects because they didn't
make it when everybody else did. Thus the new slum has a changed
spirit. Family life tends to disintegrate, identity is illusive, and there
is little hope. The Lower East Side is one of the few places where
both kinds of slums can be observed, and the difference is striking.

Perhaps the most significant fact about today's slums, and the one
with the most long-range consequences, is that they are isolated.
New walls have been erected around them which were not there
before, the walls of suburbia. We have abandoned the slums, and
that explains in part why the people who live there often feel they
have hit the dead end. That feeling is reinforced with systematic
cruelty if a slum is also a black man's ghetto.

The tragedy is that virtually nothing is being done to change this
pattern. We have not shown the faintest imagination in this respect.
We know only how to build new class ghettos. In addition to the
suburban ghettos there are new city ghettos. Some of them are
strictly private developments; others are financed by the government.
New projects are designed with ruthless efficiency to separate the
poor from the nonpoor, and usually the black from the white. On the
Lower East Side these projects have produced massive islands of
homogeneous housing, either middle-income housing or low-income
public housing. Such an approach tends to create class conflict. It
robs the affluent of a healthy contact with the poor; it stigmatizes
the poor and helps to destroy their morale. This dangerous pattern
can be changed the moment we decide to build housing that will
permit the rich and the poor to live side by side.

All of this necessitates making a monumental investment in
housing for the poor, the cost of which will be exceeded only by the
ultimate cost of not doing so.

Education

You cannot really blame a child who grows up in the sickened atmosphere of today's poverty if he becomes prematurely cynical about the value of going to school and decides that every road ahead leads to a dead end. He will begin at an early age to settle for more immediate advantages.

On the Lower East Side it often happens this way: A boy grows up in a crowded apartment where there is constant commotion. In such a setting he cannot easily learn how to concentrate, even in his 3- or 4-year-old style. Besides, he may be competing with brothers and sisters for the attention of parents who are so overwhelmed by the burden of trying to grind out an existence that they cannot adequately cope with the problem of raising children in the atmosphere of an urban slum. (There may be other complications of course, such as having an absentee father or being unwanted.) Like a majority of the children in the neighborhood, by the time he reaches the first grade (even if he has gone to kindergarten) he does not have the basic conditioning which makes him ready to learn how to read.

As a result he does not do well in school from the start. Because he does not do well and because his other problems persist, school is distasteful to him. Academically he falls progressively farther and farther behind, although perhaps neither he nor his parents realize that this is so, especially since he is doing about as well as the rest in his class. By the time he reaches the sixth grade he is nearly two years behind in reading ability. Somehow he manages to get to the eleventh grade, but he fails in mathematics and does poorly in several other subjects. He sees little value in school for the kind of work he is accustomed to think about (particularly if he is Negro or Puerto Rican), and he becomes a dropout at the age of 16, thus multiplying his chances of being stranded in a hopeless and unproductive style of life. By this time he is disillusioned. He feels he has been pushed through school and that nobody really cared that he got to be an eleventh grader in name only.

If he is a Negro, his frustration and cynicism are doubly justified. This is the sort of thing James B. Conant meant in *Slums and*

Suburbs, when he said, "We are allowing social dynamite to accumulate in our large cities."

We have concentrated minimum resources in areas of maximum need. A number of factors contribute to this situation. As the President pointed out in a message to Congress on January 12, 1965: "Our big cities generally spend only about two thirds as much per pupil as their adjacent suburbs." Conant noted that suburban communities around New York City averaged 60 professionals for every thousand pupils, while the city average is 40 to a thousand. The suburbs pay high salaries to drain off the best teachers from the city — and thereby help to insure educational poverty in depressed areas of the city. Although there is a clear determination in the suburbs "to get the best for our children," there is not a comparable determination to supply tax dollars that will prevent the children of others from getting the worst as a consequence.

The highest concentration of substitute teachers and inexperienced teachers in New York City is found in slums and ghettos, because for the same pay teachers with seniority can move to more pleasant surroundings in the city, and for higher pay they can go to the suburbs. Some stay and give heroic service, but the odds against them are formidable. When a whole classroom of children needs special help, what do you do? You end up making the most of a discouraging situation and promote children even though they can't add or read well. Besides, in such an atmosphere a teacher may be strongly disposed to underrate the potential of youngsters.

President Johnson presented these grim truths to Congress: Children of our nation's slums are usually a year behind academically by the time they reach the third grade. When they reach the eighth grade, they are up to three years behind. In depressed neighborhoods of our 15 largest cities, 60 percent of tenth-grade students drop out before finishing high school. In past generations, he said, a school dropout might have as good a chance as the next man to get ahead, but today he does not. He may be hopelessly trapped in the slums.

The classes we conduct at our church, including a remedial reading clinic twice a week, have given us occasion to witness the breakdown of education on the Lower East Side, particularly with regard to reading. Not being able to read well is a severe handicap, and a frightening handicap when you realize that in our society there is a close relationship between the inability to cope with the symbols of words and the inability to cope with life.

Children of the poor know this, even if others do not; hence their despair. Hence also the despair of the Negro parent, who fears that his child is being prepared to become an unwed mother or a bum on the street and to continue the cycle of isolation and poverty while the rest of the country moves on from riches to riches.

That's one end of the pole. On the other end is the fact that even the most gifted children of poverty, who do somehow manage to graduate from high school, rarely realize their potential. Their resources are wasted. Almost half of the million-plus public school children in New York City are Negroes and Puerto Ricans; but only 3 percent of those who attend the city's special entrance high schools, which equip top students for college, are Negroes or Puerto Ricans.

How can the cycle be broken? A great deal can and should be done through a drastic concentration of resources in areas of maximum need and by aggressive steps to integrate schools in order to offset the futility of being isolated. But we have to face the fact that as long as slums exist, the most massive efforts in schools will never be able to undo the damage being done outside of schools. To a great extent education is determined by the housing pattern. Until we have sense enough to adopt a housing policy that seeks to integrate the poor and the black with the rest of us, our boldest attempts to attack poverty through the schools will be gestures of hypocrisy.

The Cost of Poverty

We will have to decide whether we want to support poverty or get rid of it. Either way it is going to be a costly venture. There is good evidence to suggest that the cost of maintaining poverty is, in the long run, far more expensive than the cost of removing it. Selfishness will hold us all back. Even if the reverse were true, there is no moral justification for withholding from millions of Americans a decent share in the wealth of our nation.

In assessing the cost of poverty we should first of all consider what the poor pay for it.

The poor pay for poverty most of all in blood and agony — in shorter lives, sicker bodies, sicker minds; in disturbed children, bad housing, wretched education; in broken homes and illegitimate children; in futility, fear, isolation, hunger. These are costs that cannot be measured in dollars and cents by those who pay them.

The poor pay for poverty because the dollars they invest in many things bring less in return than the dollars others invest — in housing, for example, or in furniture or clothes. The poor are hurt most by taxes on essential commodities. In Chicago, if you buy a $40 suit, you pay a sales tax. If you buy a $200 hand-tailored suit, you pay no tax. The poor pay the same rates for gas and electricity that everyone else does, but the Con Edison power plant pours tons of soot on our neighborhood that people on Park Avenue never have to breathe or wash out. Poor people are much more apt to get gypped when they buy, and often they are legally fleeced. The loan that the Millers took out for $308.88 from a loan company cost them (by current rates of that firm) $99.12 when they signed up. In the end it cost them more because they had to suspend payments for several years, and the interest mounted. I could get the same loan from my bank for $29.34 interest, but the Millers could not get a bank loan. They paid more than three times as much for being poor.

The poor, however, are not the only ones who pay for poverty. A disturbed child, a youngster who goes through school but can't read beyond a fourth-grade level, a man who ruins his health on poverty — these touch the pocketbooks of all. Although the cost of such tragedies cannot be measured primarily in dollars, it is clear that the cost, translated into monetary currency, is astounding. Within walking distance of my church I can visit an immense city hospital, courts and jails, welfare centers and employment agencies — all of these jammed, and all bearing eloquent testimony to the monumental cost of maintaining poverty?

Take the problem of drug addiction. The use of narcotics is by no means limited to urban slums, but clearly that is where the problem flourishes because pushers exploit futility. According to the Rev. Edward Brown, who heads a narcotics clinic on the Lower East Side, there are at least two thousand addicts in this part of town — almost one in every hundred residents. About half of them are in jails and hospitals at any given time, and half are active. An active addict needs $10 a day to keep on the habit, and addicts are almost always compelled to steal to maintain the habit. To get his $10 he must steal $50 worth of goods a day. That would mean more than $18 million in theft each year by addicts from the Lower East Side. To a large extent it is the poor who are exploited by the pushers, muggers, and thieves, but it should be obvious that in less direct ways a circulating addict is economically costly to everyone. Of course, addicts in jails or hospitals are directly maintained at public expense.

In an area of my neighborhood that includes about 80,000 residents, 671 fires were reported during 1964. These resulted in 54 injuries, 10 deaths, and many burnt-out buildings. The cost ultimately belongs to everyone.

The New York City police arrested 13,683 children under 16 in 1964. The cost which that figure represents to the public in destruction, police protection, courts, detention centers, and training schools is only a fraction of the final price that will be exacted — purely in dollars and cents — over the years and generations.

Nowhere is the cost of poverty to the nation more dramatic than on the public welfare rolls. In June of 1964 there were 483,573 persons receiving relief from the New York City Department of Welfare, an increase of 12.4 percent over the previous June. More than half were children, and in 10 years their number had more than doubled. By the end of December — only days after a report that the nation's gross national product had gone up $40 billion in 1964 — Welfare Commissioner James R. Dumpson said that the number of persons seeking public assistance in the city was rising at the rate of about 5,850 a month, and he asked for a 1965 budget of $500 million.* This staggering announcement was less troublesome to many than reports of similar trends in the suburbs. In Nassau County the number of persons on relief has doubled since 1960, while the population went up only 6.5 percent — and in Nassau County 75 percent of those on relief are whites. A less dramatic but similar trend developed even in wealthy Westchester County, where people were shocked to learn that 8 percent of the population is living in poverty.

Up and down the line there are growing numbers of second-generation reliefers.

However the greatest economic cost of poverty is to be found not in the bills that the poor hand us (which always impress us more) but in the gains we fail to make. When there is poverty, we lose creative energy and progress on many fronts. Our resources are wasted or left undeveloped. Economists tell us that if there had been full employment in our nation during the past decade, it would have produced tens of billions of dollars in additional taxes that would have been the gain of the whole country.

We may continue to finance poverty at an accelerating price in human suffering and in dollars. Or we may decide to invest billions right now in an immense effort to lick poverty, an investment that will have to go far beyond our present token "war."

Wiping Out Poverty

We must hire the poor to create their own prosperity. We will solve the problem of poverty only if we create jobs and pay people decent wages for working. That means taking people off welfare, not putting them on. I am in basic agreement with those who say we should not just give people relief but put them to work. Putting people to work will accomplish very little if they are still given relief wages. Then we would only be satisfying our own narrow-mindedness and enabling ourselves to say, "We have taught those lazy poor a lesson or two!"—and the last state of the poor would be worse than the first. Hiring the poor to build prosperity means something more human than that.

What we need is a giant self-help program, not bigger handouts. What we need is a free market for jobs, not more restrictions. And that is why it is important for us to realize that there is no self-help program and no free market for jobs when millions of Americans are on relief, unemployed, underemployed, and underpaid. There is no free market in jobs for them because they are locked into a place where they have to settle for the nation's scrapings. We need to give the poor a chance to unlock themselves from the prison of poverty and enter freely the market of decent employment.

On the Lower East Side two staggering problems exist side by side. One is widespread unemployment. The other is dilapidated housing. At the present time we are neither creating the jobs nor building the housing for the poor. The gestures we make in those directions are not making a dent in either one. It has long impressed me as a cruel contradiction that two such problems should help-lessly stare each other in the face. With all our wealth and our technological resources, do we not have the imagination to put the two together and in some way employ the poor to construct or repair this desperately needed housing? That is the sort of thing I mean by hiring the poor to create their own prosperity.

There is good precedent for such an approach. The WPA, which began in 1935 in the heart of the Depression and lasted eight years, was a program with many faults and the butt end of countless jokes. It was controversial because it was a giant, unorthodox attempt to make jobs for people; but the WPA showed impressive accomplishments. It built highways and schools and airports; it taught people to read and made clothes for them to wear, to mention a few. Most of all, it gave work to more than 8 million Americans and supported their families, so that perhaps a quarter of our nation was directly assisted by this program. The PWA, a cousin of the WPA, helped private contractors tackle immense engineering projects like Hoover Dam and construction for the Tennessee Valley Authority. Those were expensive ventures, but history has judged them to be profoundly wise contributions to the strength and health of our country and of the world. As those programs, and later the GI Bill, bear witness, when the public invests in the future of its citizens in ways such as these, it is not engaged in a misguided give-away program, but it is enriching millions of lives and, in fact, the entire nation.

I am not suggesting a duplication of the WPA or the PWA. Nor am I suggesting that the solution is as simple as gathering all the unemployed people of the Lower East Side and putting them to work on new housing projects. I am saying, however, that we do not lack the means to lick poverty. We lack only the will. Though the frailty and resistance of human nature will not allow such a purpose to be accomplished with ease, once we have the will to do so, we can give poor people a fair, productive role in this great land and turn them loose to make a more prosperous way of life for us all.

A decision to wipe out poverty in our midst will be an expensive one, but in reality it will penalize no one because we will not be "robbing Peter to pay Paul." We will rather be investing in human resources in a way that enhances the wealth of everyone, from top to bottom, as programs like the GI Bill and the TVA have demonstrated. We will be giving the poor a chance to produce and consume, which will mean a better income for all and a fairer distribution of our wealth. I see no reason why manufacturers and retailers should not want people to become their customers.

Scarcity is no longer the problem. During the next decade automation will greatly increase the already astounding productive capacity of our nation. During the same period poverty within our borders can be virtually eliminated, if we distribute fairly what machines produce. The way to do so is in our grasp if the will to do so is present. Lacking the will, we will turn automation into a national monster.

Right now poverty at home prevents us from turning loose our full resources on the radically more cancerous sore of world poverty. If we do beat poverty at home, we can throw our full weight into a massive effort to attack world poverty. Self-interest alone may dictate this, for such an effort may be our only way of surviving as a nation in a world of "have-nots." Should we do so, it dare not take the shape of superiors putting the poor of the world on relief, but it should once again unlock people to achieve for themselves a more truly human life. The "more truly human life" is not to be defined primarily in terms of material abundance, as the last chapter of this book indicates. But neither can it belong to anyone who has this world's goods and sees his brother in need, yet closes his heart against him.

* To give the reader an idea of how these figures can explode, in December of 1965 Joseph H. Louchheim, the new Commissioner of Welfare, estimated the cost for all forms of public aid during 1965 to be about $650 million. In a letter to the author he wrote that "during October of 1965, there were 568,529 persons receiving public aid in New York City, an increase of 12.1 percent over the number in October 1964. About 60 percent were children. The number of persons receiving public assistance is rising at the rate of about 5,200 persons a month."

POLITICS AND POVERTY

One reason the Miller and the Harris families have to get along the way they do is their lack of an effective political voice. Unlike yesterday, when the poor were everywhere and politicians knew that their political power depended on representing the needs of the poor, today the poor are an isolated minority and the base of power has shifted. In the process the poor have been politically emasculated. In this chapter I want to illustrate how this is true by sketching some profiles of our neighborhood and, in particular, by describing a local urban renewal battle as it was fought and lost.

I

I moved to the Lower East Side in the spring of 1961 and was immediately struck by the housing conditions. Most of the blocks are covered by narrow 5-story tenements that house from 10 to 20 families in each building. The buildings are smack up against one another and flush to the sidewalk. They are called "old-law tenements" because they were built during the last century before a new housing law laid down specifications regarding air space, ventilation, plumbing, and the like. They are called "walk-ups" because they have no elevators. They were built for inexpensive, crowded living and have served as the starting point for just about every wave of immigrants that hit our eastern shore. That is the reason the Lower East Side is so cosmopolitan. These immigrant groups huddled in ghettos and went through all the familiar pains of being the outcasts of the land before they made their way successfully into the mainstream of American life. But they always left their traces behind, and the Lower East Side retains a sprinkling of each ethnic group — Italians, Irish, Jews, Polish, Ukrainians, Germans, Chinese, Negroes, and the most recent arrivals, the Puerto Ricans, our largest single group, who constitute more than one third of the population of Precinct Nine, where I live. This precinct is smaller than one square mile but claims more than a hundred thousand residents.

The streets are busy streets, alive with people when the weather is warm. The streets are also dirty. They always bear the traces of garbage that never quite made it from the battered cans to the sanitation trucks. Sometimes it seems that both the people and the debris on the streets have oozed out of the tenements, and in a sense that is so.

Most of the tenements have not been maintained properly, though their internal condition varies considerably. Two buildings side by side may look almost identical from the street. Inside, one is relatively well kept, while the one next to it attacks you with the smell of urine and other odors. The plaster may be cracked, the stairs unsteady, and obscene words scratched and scrawled on the walls. The apartments, too, can be attractive and livable or depressing, depending on the intention of the landlord and the resources of the tenants.

Low-income public housing projects accommodate about 15,000 people on the eastern side of the precinct along the East River. North of the precinct is a giant middle-income housing development owned and operated by Metropolitan Life Insurance Company, but it is separated from the precinct both by its affluence and by 14th Street, a wide and heavily traveled boulevard.

Most of the buildings in the tenement area are solid, but violations of the building code are common — defective plumbing, no heat, rats, and the like. These violations go unchecked because we have made slum real estate a profitable business. For a variety of reasons the way to make money on these buildings is to have many apartments, invest as little cash in them as possible for maintenance, and let the rents go as high as New York's rent control will allow. Since landlords are permitted an automatic 15 percent increase every time there is a change of tenants in an apartment, it can be lucrative to encourage a rapid turnover of tenants, and unscrupulous landlords have ways of arranging that, sometimes by direct harassment.

Of course there are laws that require landlords to meet minimum standards in maintaining a building, but these laws are seldom enforced. First of all, a tenant must file an official complaint with the city, and many do not know how to file or are afraid of reprisal from the landlord. Second, if a complaint is filed, let us say with the Department of Buildings, it may be one or two years before an inspector comes out to check the alleged violation, since the staff is always inadequate and there is always a massive backlog of complaints.

If a landlord is charged by the city with a violation, he must be found before a summons can be issued. Most of the landlords are absentee landlords, and some of them are experts at evading the court. One newspaper item, dated August 1962, tells of a landlord from Long Beach, Long Island, who was chased by the city for three years. He was finally handed a summons in the lavatory of his office building by process servers who hid there and waited 60 hours for him!

Even if the landlord is summoned to court, there is usually not much to worry about because the penalty is mild—something like a license to violate the law. A landlord who is fined $85 for a building with 100 violations may justifiably consider himself rewarded by such an arrangement. And if a landlord is compelled to spend money clearing up violations, he usually has dozens or hundreds of other buildings to make up for such losses many times over.

It would be a mistake, however, to single out the landlord and lay all the blame on his doorstep while ignoring the banks who support him, the political establishment which is much more responsive to his real estate interests than to human suffering, and our own apathy which permits all this to happen. A reporter once told me: "Landlords ought to be given medals. They are the heroes in this housing mess. They are heroes because they offer themselves as society's scapegoat. We blame them for everything and get rid of our own guilt in allowing this kind of situation to exist."

Late in the summer of 1961, when Mayor Robert Wagner was waging a battle in the primary campaign to retain his job, he walked through parts of our neighborhood. By arrangement he visited one of the old tenement buildings on East Fourth Street and was appropriately indignant at the conditions he saw. Mayors of New York, it should be mentioned, have provided the city with much eloquence on the problem of housing, especially before elections. This time Wagner promised immediate action, and in

August of 1961 (just before the primary balloting) an Area Service
Project office was established. Its purpose was to provide intensive
inspection of all buildings in 24 of the worst blocks of the
precinct. The idea was to send a team of inspectors into each
building, comprehensively report all violations, and follow these
through the courts, if necessary, until they are removed. The staff of
the Area Services Project office has done exceptionally fine work,
but its effort only illustrates how remiss the city normally is in its
treatment of slum housing. Even though the Area Services Project is
an emergency, intensive effort to speed up inspection and remove
violations, by March of 1965 — 3½ years after the project began —
the Buildings Department had completed the equivalent of 6 of the
24 blocks, with violations cleared on about half of the inspected
buildings. The Health Department had completed inspection of
about nine blocks. It is possible to appreciate the work of these
public servants from Area Services and still distinguish from it the
indifference of the city when it comes to slum housing.

The picture on housing is not entirely bad in these old-law
tenements. Many buildings are quite livable, and that is a tribute to
those owners who have consciences and to the people who often do
astoundingly well under discouraging circumstances. The general
situation is bad enough, however, to make the visitor or newcomer to
our neighborhood conclude that these tenements ought to be torn
down and new housing constructed, the sooner the better. I was
no exception.

II

In July of 1961, only a few months after moving to the Lower East
Side, I was asked to take part in a meeting of representatives from
neighborhood agencies. We were told that the city had designated
a 3-block site, which it called the Tompkins Square Housing Site, as
suitable for urban renewal. It was an area composed largely of old,
small industrial shops and only 165 apartments. A representative
of the city's Housing and Redevelopment Board (HRB) was on hand
to urge that neighborhood leaders participate with the city in working out a suitable plan for this 3-block site.

I must admit I was impressed with the attitude of this HRB
official toward our neighborhood. She made it clear that "citizen

participation" is one of the federal requirements which must be met by the city in order to receive urban renewal funds. The city wanted to find out from neighborhood people what we needed and wanted.

To illustrate how the poor lack political "savvy," I later found out that on May 1, when the chairman of the City Planning Commission announced the Tompkins Square Housing Site as suitable for urban renewal, he had simultaneously announced similar plans for an area two miles across town in the West Village. The reaction in the two communities was not the same. The West Village immediately thundered its vote of disapproval at the city's intention and, led by Jane Jacobs, the *Village Voice,* and other articulate spokesmen, virtually inundated the Board of Estimate with its protest. The project was dropped. Meanwhile there was nothing but silence in our neighborhood. We didn't even know what was going on. Partly as a result of West Village opposition the HRB (Housing and Redevelopment Board) was eager for a smooth relationship with our neighborhood and had suggested this meeting to request citizen participation.

Out of this request the Tompkins Square Housing Committee formed and began to hold public meetings. We recognized a need for renewal, and we took at face value the clearly expressed wishes of the HRB for community participation. We naively assumed from official assurances that a genuine dialog would develop between the neighborhood and the city.

Such dialog was never to take place.

At first we heard housing experts explain the options open to us. Meanwhile five members of our committee interviewed most of the residents on the proposed site and came up with information that included the following:

Tenants paid a median rental of $36.50 per apartment, or an
   average of $10.08 per room a month.
Nearly half of the apartments were overcrowded.
Half of the family units had incomes of less than $3,000 a year.
Nearly three fourths of the tenants said they would like to live
   in the new apartments, provided the rents were low enough.
About half of the residents were Puerto Ricans, and the other half were of European background, plus a handful of Negroes. Many

of the European-background people were old folks who had lived there for decades. While the HRB's own survey taken later showed less pessimistic income figures (e. g., 37 percent of the families with incomes below $3,000), the picture was essentially the same. We were impressed by the low incomes of the people, by the low rentals which they paid, and by the number of those who wanted to remain on the site, provided they could afford the rent.

Then Robert Dennis, a member of our committee and a city planner (though not in the employ of the city), together with another city planner and an architect, formed a team which made a building-by-building examination, not only of the 3-block site but also of another 8 blocks immediately to the west and adjoining the site. They designated each building in one of three categories: (1) structurally solid and not in need of repair; (2) structurally solid, but in need of code enforcement; and (3) dilapidated buildings which should be demolished within 10 years. The results showed that almost all the buildings — both on and off the proposed site — fit into category 2.

With this information to go on we were able to piece together a kind of proposal that used this logic:

1. Recognizing that most of the people on the site and in the adjoining blocks had very low incomes, we asked that new housing though including middle-income units, be built primarily for the people of the area at rentals they could afford.

2. Most of the apartments on the site were situated in two clusters of buildings on one corner of the site. Since many tenants had incomes so low that they could not afford the rentals even of new low-income public housing (which were then coming in at $16-$18 a room), or for other reasons might not be eligible for public housing, we asked the city to redraw the boundary of the proposed site to exclude those buildings from the site. Besides, the supply of low-rent housing in the city is desperately short, and we felt it would be a mistake to further deplete that supply unless absolutely necessary.

3. We asked that the site be treated not as an isolated area but in relation to the surrounding blocks, so that this renewal program could become the first phase of a series of stages to upgrade and

replace housing without displacing large numbers of residents from the neighborhood.

4. We suggested that renewal, in its various stages, not simply bulldoze blocks wholesale but pursue a more selective course to preserve the most habitable buildings, and construct new houses, including perhaps some row houses, in "vest pocket" sections.

Although we were limited by lack of personnel, time, and funds, we were able to pick up widespread support for our proposal in the neighborhood. Our neighborhood council, the Housing Division of LENA (Lower Eastside Neighborhoods Association), Puerto Rican and civil rights organizations, and other community groups supported our proposal, and it was clear that the great majority of neighborhood people who have no institutional voice were also responding favorably to our approach. Even the local Democratic organization, a stronghold of Tammany Hall, promised support — which was later retracted, presumably under pressure from the city.

Already it was becoming evident that while the HRB was ready to fill us in on the most general sort of information regarding procedure, there was no willingness to exchange ideas of substance. We met with Milton Mollen, chairman of the HRB, and board members on several occasions, and we were always received with courtesy. But we had no idea what the city planners were producing for the HRB, nor were we allowed access to their thinking. As the chief of the Project Development for the HRB said at a meeting with us in August 1962, the technicians did not want someone from the neighborhood "peeking over our shoulders."

We began to grow increasingly alarmed over HRB silence. A new community affairs man assigned to us by the HRB insisted that as soon as the "preliminary concept" of the HRB was ready, then the neighborhood committee could sit down with the board and discuss matters of substance. He assured us over and over again that the preliminary concept would be "only the most tentative sort of sketch."

At HRB headquarters in December 1962 Chairman Mollen unveiled what he announced to be not the preliminary concept but "the tentative final concept." It ignored the key priorities urged by the community and proposed instead a straight middle-income development of 900 units, with rents up to $30 a room, but with the possibility of as many as 20 percent of the units skewed down to $18 a room—still out of range for most of the site tenants. Mollen emphasized that the HRB wanted to speed it on to Washington for approval as quickly as possible.

On Jan. 10, 1963, an open meeting was held at Public School 61 on East 12th Street. The entire neighborhood was invited to hear both plans presented on an equal-time basis. HRB chairman Mollen and his staff members did so on behalf of the city. Nearly 300 persons (a phenomenal turnout in our neighborhood) listened to both proposals and asked questions, after which a motion from the floor to back the neighborhood plan rather than the city's proposal carried with only four dissenting votes—although there were no doubt other dissenters present.

The expression of the community by this time could not have been more evident, but even that elicited no readiness on the part of the HRB to discuss serious differences. The HRB continued to use the enormous resources and personnel at its disposal to garner support for its concept in the face of a clear neighborhood consensus to the contrary. They did so chiefly by contacting and soliciting support from a number of groups, most of which had leadership north of 14th Street and who might therefore be prone to favor middle-income housing as a way of upgrading the area.

All of this impressed me as a violation of people who had much at stake, but who carried little political weight. It was small comfort to learn that our experience was not unique, but part of a pattern that affected other neighborhoods of the city.

Some of the opposition seemed crass and ruthless. I mentioned before the regular Democratic organization (the Jefferson Club), which first endorsed, then opposed us. The leadership of this club (like that of the neighborhood Republican club) resided not in Precinct Nine tenements but in the well-heeled area north of 14th Street. That organization's endorsement came one evening a few days before a primary election in 1962. The district leader let me speak to perhaps a hundred assembled captains and election workers. They cheered our proposal—and I have no doubt most of them meant it. The district leader then publicly praised the

proposal and assured our committee of the club's backing. I was
elated. But after the election no written endorsement was forth-
coming, and soon it became evident that the district leader was
opting for the HRB's proposal.

While the HRB was garnering support, the Jefferson Club held
a "public" meeting, to which — I saw by surprise in a newspaper —
neighborhood groups had received written invitations to send representatives. That should have read "selected" neighborhood groups,
because those known to favor our plan were not invited. Several
of us went to the meeting anyway, but were barred from attending,
until the chairman of the HRB arrived and suggested we be permitted to enter. Inside we sat quietly all evening, because despite
spontaneous questions from the floor, the man who chaired the
meeting would not permit even the HRB chairman to explain the
neighborhood's proposal or the reasons for opposition to the city's
plan. As that club knew, it did not dare to hold an open
meeting on this matter because the neighborhood viewpoint was
clear.

Much of our opposition came from well-meaning men who seemed
incapable of putting themselves in the shoes of our neighbors.
After repeated invitations the chief of Project Development of the
HRB agreed to tour the site and visit a few apartments with us. We
visited one elderly Jewish lady who showed us her home. Everything
looked old inside, but it was clean and well kept. "It's not the
best," she said, "but it's home. Where else would I go?" We
talked out in the hallway of her building downstairs for a while,
but what impressed our city official most seemed to be a garbage
can in the hall and a cockroach that scooted along the wall and
almost got on his shoulder. Repeatedly the HRB officials would wax
indignant about the "rat- and roach-infested slums" which they
wanted to remove. They had a point, and living as they did in far
better conditions, they were probably saying what they honestly
believed; but they never seemed to be able to see through the eyes
of the poor and understand that an old, small place is better than
no place at all. Nor could any of them suggest what could be done
to house the poor removed by urban renewal other than to crowd
them into the already diminishing supply of low-income housing.

This illustrates the strongest argument against urban renewal as now conceived, namely, that it usually destroys low-income housing and fails to replace it because it is basically in the business of middle-income housing. The net effect is that the slums are not eliminated by urban renewal but simply shifted and spread, so that despite massive housing construction in New York the problem of the slums gets progressively worse, not better. For every slum it destroys New York creates two new ones.

Top officials of the HRB consistently admitted to us, and on occasion said publicly, that the third of the city's population with no place to go is the third with incomes of less than $4,000 a year, precisely those citizens whose needs were being bypassed in this urban renewal venture. These same officials admitted with equal candor that they had no solution for the problem of low-income housing. Such honesty impressed us but clearly offered no acceptable way out. Officials appealed to the need for middle-income housing in Manhattan and asked us to look at the city as a whole, not just at our own neighborhood. The city's need for more suitable middle-income housing and for higher tax returns cannot be denied. However, when such needs consistently take priority and ride roughshod over the obviously more urgent needs of others, one can be forgiven if he fails to be persuaded by those arguments. They give the poor little to cheer about. In the last analysis they prove to be another instance of the welfare state operating for the benefit not of the most needy, who no longer swing much political weight, but of those who are fashionably middle class and of interests such as real estate and the construction industry, which stand to reap immense profits from such ventures.

Another aspect that concerned us deeply is the history of discrimination against Negroes and Puerto Ricans to which urban renewal has played partner. It is not because of misunderstanding but because of suffering that some have called urban renewal "urban removal" or "Negro removal." Since our whole pattern of discrimination has forced Negroes and Puerto Ricans into slums and ghettos, they find themselves living in precisely those areas which the city designates as blighted and suitable for urban renewal. Charles Abrams, writing in Commentary (January 1963) on "The

Housing order and Its Limits," said:

> With the advent of urban renewal after 1949, moreover, racial dis-
> crimination with federal blessing took on an additional form in the
> wholesale evictions of Negroes from footholds they had established in the
> cities. Negroes constituted more than seventy percent of those dis-
> placed from their homes to make room for more expensive housing de-
> velopments (all financed in part by federal aid); and a high proportion
> of the remaining thirty percent were Puerto Ricans, Orientals, and other
> minorities. Here too, the federal housing agencies ruled that both dis-
> placement and refusal to rent space in the new federally aided projects
> to minorities were matters of local option.

Some opted against discrimination, of course, and in any event
President Kennedy's Executive Order of Nov. 20, 1963, banning discrimination in federally aided housing, put an end (at least
legally) to the practice of refusing to rent to Negroes and others
for racial or ethnic reasons. However, that was never the chief form
of discrimination in urban renewal. The chief form was economic
because it displaced minority group people (in our instance,
Puerto Ricans) who were not able to pay rents in the new buildings.
Thus on the Lower East Side, which is both racially mixed and pre-
dominantly low income, the thousands of middle-income housing
units that urban renewal has produced have virtually no Negro
or Puerto Rican residents. These projects have become less a means
of giving "balance" to the area than a way of producing islands
of imbalance. Our committee was understandably concerned about
the perpetuation of this pattern in our instance.

I have already said that the HRB was able to secure support from
organizations (including one church and several synagogs) whose
leadership resided above 14th Street. Two fall in a different category and deserve special mention. One was the board of directors of
the Lower Eastside Neighborhoods Association (LENA). Our neighborhood council, which is one of four neighborhood councils making
up LENA, endorsed the committee's plan and opposed the city. So
did the Housing Division of LENA. But the board of directors of that
organization is dominated by people who can be classified as
representing the interest of middle-income cooperatives and
business on the southeastern part of the Lower East Side. They have

generally favored middle-income housing over the needs of low-income people. Organized in terms of power from the top down and not from the bottom up, LENA illustrates how spokesmen for the poor tend to be people who do not always represent them favorably.

A similar instance was endorsement of the HRB proposal by the Borough President's Planning Board for the Lower East Side. This board has advisory power only, but as a group of leaders that ostensibly represents the people of the area its voice carries some weight. Even more so than LENA, the board is controlled by political, commercial, and middle-income housing interests. (Some are members of both boards.) I was appointed to this board, I was told, as a way of giving "balance" to that body, but there is no balance in sight. Again the poor are shortchanged in such an arrangement.

When the HRB announced its "tentative final" concept and began systematically rounding up support for that concept, there was no longer any question about being in dialog with the city. Officials went through some of the motions. The Borough President paid a surprise visit to our parish house, but it was to explain, not to listen. Robert Dennis (our city planner) and I learned of one minor concession in May 1963 in a final meeting with the chairman and board members of the HRB (a proposal to include 200 units that would rent possibly as low as $18 to $20 a room),* but this could hardly be confused with dialog. As a result we were left with no alternative but to oppose the city plan. We corresponded with Robert C. Weaver and officials of the Housing and Home Finance Agency, protesting in particular that the city had failed to meet the requirement of citizen participation. The reply was that the mayor's Citizens Advisory Committee had reviewed and approved the HRB concept and therefore the legal stipulation had been met. It was the first time I heard that such a committee existed. They probably had never heard of us either, and we certainly had no opportunity to present our ideas to them. After all the promises about citizen participation we received from the HRB, this small group of well-to-do citizens, all quite removed from our neighborhood, suddenly became the authorized vehicle for that participation. We felt we had been made victims of citizen manipulation.

We fought the HRB at City Hall in public hearings before the City Planning Commission and the Board of Estimate. We were able to produce more speakers than our opponents — and if speakers who resided outside the neighborhood had been disqualified, our strength would have been far more apparent.

We lost. But we gave the city a hard time and hammered home a point: The poor must become our first concern in housing, not our last concern.

III

Using the particular problem of housing, I have been trying to illustrate the fact that the poor are politically voiceless and the last to be listened to. I have had occasion to mention a large, private, middle-income housing development north of 14th Street called Stuyvesant Town. The relation of Stuyvesant Town to the area south of 14th Street is a modern classic example of evils that are showered upon the poor in and through housing because they are politically expendable.

Stuyvesant Town covers 18 city blocks and houses 22,405 people according to the 1960 census. Until the end of World War II those blocks were an extension of the old, dilapidated tenement houses south of 14th Street. Not only a busy street but economic and racial factors and mutual suspicion separate residents below and above 14th Street. People who live in Stuyvesant Town usually do not like to go south of 14th Street to shop or visit or attend church. Not many of them send children to school south of 14th Street, but to vastly superior schools west of the development. They are afraid and disgusted by what they see below 14th Street. A local paper that circulates every apartment in Stuyvesant Town encourages such fear in dramatizing the most sordid features of the tenement area and speaks in glaring headlines of the young hoodlums and punks below 14th Street who attack or rob people in Stuyvesant Town. On the other hand, people south of 14th Street do not know their neighbors to the north. They are not welcome to play on the streets or play-grounds of Stuyvesant Town because it is private property watched by uniformed guards. Fourteenth Street is sometimes called "The Barrier."

In 1940 about 15,000 people lived in those blocks. Most of them were poor. In 1943, under a new state law and by contract with the city, Metropolitan Life Insurance Company agreed to buy the land from the city at a drastically depreciated price. The city was willing to bear the loss on this in return for anticipated gains in property tax later on. The bulldozers moved in, and thousands of families were evacuated. Hardly any of them were rehoused in the new buildings that were completed between 1947 and 1949.

Metropolitan Life made Stuyvesant Town middle class and white, reflecting a strong impulse to create a suburban community in Manhattan, a non-city city. In keeping with the mood of the 1940s it openly discriminated against Negroes until pressure from the City Council led Metropolitan Life to admit three Negro families in 1950. An ordinance passed by the City Council the following year made discrimination in such projects illegal. However, according to the 1960 census — a decade after Stuyvesant Town agreed to integrate — only 47 persons from a total population of 22,405 were Negroes, or barely two tenths of 1 percent. If one includes the 16 Puerto Ricans, that would raise the integration percentage to almost three tenths of one percent, or a little less than three Negroes and Puerto Ricans out of every thousand residents!

In creating Stuyvesant Town several things happened. First, thousands of people, most of them poor, had to move off the property. The cancer of slums spread elsewhere. Second, the new housing units were not only economically stratified, but racially restrictive as well. Even more is at stake, however; for injustice has a way of reaching out in all directions. Consider the matter of education.

Since the latter part of 1963, when long-overdue pressure for quality and integrated schools in New York suggested the possibility of exchanging more children in both directions across 14th Street, a furor was created by parents in Stuyvesant Town and elsewhere above 14th Street. In public meetings many residents spoke self-righteously of conditions below 14th Street, but very few stopped to consider that the statistics I have noted speak eloquently in laying some of the responsibility on themselves. Those citizens defended indignantly the sanctity of the neighborhood school, and one can appreciate the argument that integration by sending and receiving pupils outside specified boundaries can be artificial. What must not be ignored, however, is that "natural" integration can occur in schools only when the housing pattern of a neighborhood is one of integration. If a project like Stuyvesant Town systematically excludes people, and if the residents of that project exclude themselves from responsibility toward the misery of neighbors whose community they have invaded, is it fair to blame the excluded ones for conditions that are characteristic of crowded ghettos? Or to be surprised that Negroes and Puerto Ricans and others are desperate for a break in this ugly pattern? One may ask what price also Stuyvesant Town residents ultimately pay in moral currency for living in a middle-class ghetto. What we see happening in Stuyvesant Town is precisely the same flight from reality represented by most suburban communities.

Unlike the area below 14th Street, Stuyvesant Town is to be reckoned with politically. I have already noted that in the regular political organizations of my election district, leadership resided in Stuyvesant Town. Of its 22,405 inhabitants, 13,474 Stuyvesant Town residents voted in the 1964 presidential election, just about its full complement of eligible voters. By comparison, in the area of the then same Assembly District south of 14th Street, only 7,224 voted in that election although its population of 35,420 is considerably larger than that of Stuyvesant Town. Besides this, residents of Stuyvesant Town clearly show far greater political strength in terms of financial resources, organization, and ability to articulate their desires. As a result Stuyvesant Town carries a disproportionately strong voice in the decision-making process, as effective blocking of any school pairing demonstrated.

Such a situation lends itself to a certain amount of hypocrisy. In the 1964 election campaign, at a large public gathering north of 14th Street, the two candidates for the General Assembly were asked if they thought Stuyvesant Town discriminated in housing. I can hardly believe anyone in the audience had any real doubts about the matter. The incumbent answered that he did not think so, and although his answer evoked some laughter, it was clear that the audience was generally pleased. The losing challenger said in a careful statement that he did not think he would have had the same chance of becoming a resident of Stuyvesant Town if his skin had been black. His reply not only displeased many in the audience, but for it he was ridiculed in the *Town and Village* newspaper. His answer may have cost him the election.

Speaking of elections, it should be noted that sometimes the un-explainable irony of politics also works to the detriment of the poor. In 1965 a young, freshman state senator began representing the Lower East Side. He was the choice of the party regulars and was promptly rewarded with a chairmanship — of the State Senate committee on agriculture!

In all of this it is easy to see that the political cards are often stacked against the poor, whose voices are muted and whose needs can be minimized or postponed.

IV

On the eastern edge of Precinct Nine is a large strip of low-income public housing (Jacob Riis and Lillian Wald projects) with a population total of approximately 15,000. This figure includes about an equal number of Negro, Puerto Rican, and Caucasian tenants. Rents range from $11 to $18 a room per month in these two projects, with the rent based on income, number of dependents in a family, and other factors.

Stuyvesant Town represents one form of discrimination against the poor. The Jacob Riis and Lillian Wald projects in some respects also represent a form of discrimination against the poor, although such projects were obviously conceived and are operated for the benefit of low-income families.

To many, public housing represents their only live option for decent housing, and critics of public housing should not forget that. At the present time there is a backlog of 120,000 applicants for public housing in the city of New York. There are no doubt tens of thousands of others who would like to apply for public housing but are discouraged because of the massive backlog. Only 10 per-cent of the applicants make it in any given year. Some do not apply because they cannot afford even the lowest rents in public housing, and some cannot qualify because of such factors as illegitimate children or incidence of crime in the family.

In some respects public housing is sick. It is sick primarily because it dumps low-income families into one economically (and often racially) segregated pile. There is nothing intrinsically bad about poor people living together. It is bad, however, when they are systematically excluded from living with others, and when 15,000 people are legally penalized by constantly draining off their most economically successful families and their leadership. This happens because, to qualify for public housing, one must not earn more than a specified income (depending upon family size, etc.). Thus the most stable and helpful members of such developments — precisely those who are best situated to help it achieve some sense of community — are continually being evicted. So we see that public housing, along with urban renewal and the postwar rush to suburbia, partakes of the deadening inability to get away from our neo-ghetto mentality, which is inflexibly committed to one-class living.

The most obvious result of this situation in public housing is that the slums tend to invade these projects. Urine in the elevators, scratched-up walls, and crime all bear convincing testimony to the fact that even when the poor are grouped in *this* kind of ghetto, a high price is being paid for isolating them. Tenants have to take the onus with the bonus, for such projects become stigmatized, and residents are often made to feel less than human for living there.

There is a less obvious result of public housing's policy of evicting leadership. Politically the poor are robbed of some of their strongest spokesmen and best organizers. They have to leave, and because of various factors they are encouraged to seek housing in a stratified middle-income area and become part of the pattern of escape from the problems out of which they emerged. Perhaps, like the Israelites who were admonished repeatedly never to forget that they were once strangers and slaves in Egypt, these aspiring and successful residents in public housing want to forget their roots and find their identity elsewhere. And once they have isolated them-selves from their former neighbors, they cannot be expected to retain their sympathy for the suffering they once knew — and even if they do, they are usually too far away to do much about it. One outcome of this is that the poor, kept in isolation and with only a whisper of a political voice, can be largely bypassed when public policy is made.

V

So far in this chapter on politics and poverty I have dealt almost exclusively with the matter of housing in our area. Much more evidence in this field could be introduced. It should be understood, however, that politics and poverty meet for unfair encounter on a host of other fields as well. Let me cite two instances which do not revolve only around the matter of housing.

During the last several years a controversy has raged over the proposed construction of a Lower Manhattan expressway that would cut across Manhattan and slice through the Lower East Side. Whether or not such an expressway is needed remains a highly controversial and much-debated point. Among other things, construction of the expressway will involve destruction of housing for 2,000 low-income families. In this instance almost all groups from Lower Manhattan, including many voices that are not normally concerned about low-income housing, have opposed the expressway because approximately 800 small businesses and 10,000 jobs are at stake and because the expressway would physically divide neighborhoods.

The city is tempted because the expressway would be part of an interstate highway, and 90 percent of the cost would be supplied by the federal government. But one reason — many believe the key reason — the expressway has been pushed so energetically and finally approved is great pressure from labor unions of the construction industry to open up more jobs for construction workers. Civil rights leaders are especially irked by this pressure from trade unions because those unions, representing well-salaried skills, have had a notorious record of excluding Negroes. Therefore one type of argument used by proponents of the expressway looks morally self-incriminating if considered from the standpoint of those who have been denied an adequate share of our nation's abundance: "The route of the proposed expressway passes through a depressed and deteriorating area with markedly low property values. Much of it is a wretched slum. It is a valley of blight amidst mountains of prosperity." **

Even if the case for the expressway is as clear as its supporters maintain, the fact remains that it stands as a disturbing example of how politics and public funds tend to move (often with the finest of logic) for the benefit of the well-to-do (construction companies, construction workers, car owners, trucking firms) and at the expense of the poor, whose homes would be torn down, their jobs destroyed, and their neighborhoods divided.

Another example is Mobilization for Youth. MFY was initiated on the Lower East Side in May 1962 as the nation's first massive assault of its type on juvenile delinquency and, more broadly, on poverty. Financed as a multi-million-dollar experiment by federal, city, and private funds, MFY tries to get at some of the causes of failure among young people in the neighborhood. It trains young people for jobs and finds employment for them. It hires teen-agers who are doing well in school to assist children who are having difficulty. It tries to get nonjoiners to participate in constructive group activities of various types.

One thing that MFY seemed to sense from the outset was that the problem of delinquency is not an isolated matter, apart from the whole context of a life which fosters delinquency. MFY moved inevitably and increasingly into the area we can broadly call social and political action. It encouraged tenants living in run-down buildings to organize and insist on their legal rights. People who were frustrated because of racial or ethnic discrimination were encouraged to give constructive expression to their feelings in civil rights demonstrations.

As MFY moved into the area of social action, protests against it mounted. That is understandable. In developing leadership among the people of the neighborhood (many of them previously cynical or apathetic or accustomed to underestimating themselves) and encouraging action that involved various challenges to the establishment, MFY was working for a type of reform which many of its early proponents — themselves part of the establishment — had not bargained for. In January 1964 a number of public school principals protested that MFY helped organize Puerto Rican mothers who were unhappy over lack of textbooks for their youngsters. These long-submissive mothers sometimes expressed their frustrations to school officials in ways that showed a lack of dignity.

Rent strikes were another sore spot. This is a legal procedure, not

often used, of withholding rent from a landlord when there are
serious violations that go unattended, and depositing it with the
court. When the repairs are completed, the rent is turned over to the
landlord. Taking advantage of this procedure usually requires the
service of an attorney, and when MFY began offering free legal
advice and services, tenants were encouraged to take action,
action that was often embarrassing to officials because it exposed
ignored misery.

Criticism also hit when some of the MFY-organized groups par-
ticipated in a one-day school boycott that protested against the
segregated and inferior schools abounding in New York.

At last these protests erupted into widely publicized and almost
wholly unsubstantiated charges of leftist infiltration, as the New
York Times pointed out in editorials. MFY's activities were particularly galling to those who thought (correctly) that they were giving
money that was being used to criticize and even undermine them.
The Times quoted Mitchell Ginsberg, associate dean of the Columbia
University School of Social Work: "If I were the Mayor, how would
I feel about giving money to an agency that might turn around and
be highly critical of my welfare department or my school system?"

Resentment on the part of local leaders was sometimes apparent.
Michael Bloom, the Democratic leader of the Fourth Assembly District, said that the Lower East Side had lived in harmony for years,
and he didn't like to have the MFY people come in and unsettle
things. "They should just take care of the youth and stop getting
into some of this other nonsense the Red infiltrators started steaming
up, like rent strikes and boycotts," the Times quoted him as saying.

After several investigations and a good deal of harassment from
some elements of the press and some officials, MFY went on with its
work, but smarting from criticism and with the admonition to work
more closely with neighborhood leaders and city officials. The net
effect of this is yet to be seen. It does demonstrate, however, the
innate reluctance of politics to work for the best interests of the
poor, even when it is ostensibly serving them.

For the first time a minority, America's poor, have been largely bypassed by our nation's growing wealth. Isolated as never before
in ghettos of poverty, abandoned by yesterday's poor who now

live separate lives in new middle-class ghettos, the poor find themselves outside the mainstream of concern. Like Samson, they have
been shorn of their strength and left to tread the mill.

Often we do not allow them even that dignity.

* Late in 1965 it was announced by the HRB that the number of these moderately
priced units, financed under Section 221-d-3 of the National Housing Act, was
increased from 200 to 370 — but with estimated average rentals of $26.50 per room.
Thus a one-bedroom apartment will rent for $106 to $111 per month, plus utilities.

** From the opening statement by Charles F. Preusse on behalf of the Triborough
Bridge and Tunnel Authority before the Board of Estimate, Dec. 22, 1964.

RICH CHURCH, POOR CHURCH

A. POVERTY AND THE ANTICHURCH

So far this book has been intended for Americans in general.
A particular word to Americans who claim to have a special calling
as believers in Jesus Christ is in order, for in some very basic ways
Christians seem to be contradicting the Gospel they confess.
Although it is not possible for us to detach ourselves from human
need and still be Christians, in some respects the church has
systematically excluded itself from such need. When Christians do so,
they are turning the church into a demonic enterprise of self-
concern. The general attitude of Christians toward people of
poverty illustrates the extent to which this has already happened.

The Church Is out of Touch with Poverty

After the Christmas Eve services at Trinity, two young men took toys
to children in homes where we had reason to believe there would be
no presents to open. One of them brought some toys to several
young boys in a Puerto Rican family. The boys greeted this
unexpected arrival with pure joy and excitement, but the way they
had of expressing their emotion was to run around the tiny
apartment shouting obscene words.

We have a hard time visualizing a situation like that, but it
should remind us how removed the church is from the poor of our
land. This removal is not only evident in our lack of personal
encounter with the poor. On a broader scale it is most clearly seen
in the flight of the church from crowded, decaying residential
sections of our cities.

Trinity Lutheran Church, which I serve, is on Manhattan's Lower
East Side. During a period of time in which some 200,000 people
were moving into Manhattan below 14th Street, 17 Protestant
churches moved out and many others, like Trinity, dwindled to
a handful of old faithfuls. Such statistics have led the *Annals of the
American Academy of Political and Social Science* (November
1960) to observe: "There appears to be something in the Urban
Community and its culture which is alien, if not hostile, to the
church." The truth of course is not that the city is hostile to the

church but that the church has largely abandoned the poor inner-core areas of the city.

The pattern is the same in every city. While America becomes more and more an urbanized society, city churches are dying and thus removing themselves from the mainstream of American life. From 1920 to 1960, 44 Lutheran churches within two miles of the heart of Detroit were reduced to four — even though during this 44-year period the Protestant population of that same area increased. The "wrong" kind of people moved in. Many of them were poor and black.

We are out of touch.

That is what makes it possible for the suburban Christian to work in the city but feel no sense of responsibility toward the city — its taxes, its tenements, its unequal and inadequate schools. Being out of touch makes it possible for him to take nightly refuge in surroundings that have nothing in common with the slums, to do nothing about it and feel no discomfort.

That makes it possible for the Christian to wonder why Negroes make such a stir over the civil rights issue and to be annoyed when they do not show more patience. He is out of touch with their suffering.

That is why so many Christians can think only in outrageous stereotypes about the poor and imagine that the overarching reason why people are on welfare is laziness.

"We only know what we read in the papers, and it makes us afraid and disgusted," a lady explains. What an indictment against us! Are we so distant from human agony and so unaware that our distance is nourishing the very thing we abhor? Should we laugh or cry when people say they are afraid to visit or even drive through the Lower East Side?

The main problem our nation faces in attacking poverty is the indifference of the people who might read a book like this one. News analyst James Reston writes regarding the war on poverty: "In every city and community there seems to be a small group of leaders who believe the job can be done and who are helping, but most people still seem to be sticking to the old Biblical idea that 'Ye have the poor always with you.'" (New York Times, Jan. 10, 1965)

Many Christians undoubtedly cite those words of Jesus to prove that nothing can be done. Aside from the fact this attitude misrepresents our Lord's intention concerning the poor, it shows how out of touch we have become. And we plant most of our new congregations where we will be almost certain to stay out of touch as long as possible.

We Are Committed to a Middle Class Style of Life

That the church is out of touch with the poor of our land is not merely a problem of ignorance but one of deliberate commitment. Christians, like others, choose willfully to be aloof from human need. We consciously remove ourselves from the problem of poverty by the manner in which we become committed to a middle-class style of life.

We are dedicated to the pursuit of material comforts. For most of us the American dream includes a home of our own, a late-model car, a hi-fi set, and a closetful of clothes we probably throw away before they wear out. It includes security for retirement and enough pin money to take trips, go bowling, and buy cosmetics without ever really feeling a pinch. There is nothing intrinsically wrong with these things — if they do not hinder us from ministering to people who are deprived of much more basic commodities.

"He who has two coats, let him share with him who has none." The words of John sometimes come to my mind when I speak in suburban congregations. I know well enough that coat-sharing usually consists of throwing it in a box for world relief when we are ready for a new one. John didn't mean that. Perhaps in our more complicated society he would have suggested a comparable expenditure toward removing causes of injustice or unemployment so that poor people could have a fairer portion of the necessities of life — which a coat represented in the first-century language of John. Our coats could do much more than keep a handful of people warm; their value, perhaps exchanged in the currency of young parish workers for an inner-city congregation, could open up worlds of love for others. Is it too much to expect that if a Christian means business he will be willing to invest as much in eliminating poverty and in the church's mission to the poor as he puts on his back — not for warmth, but for the extras: the fur coat, the second suit, the jewelry, etc.? If not, how will we be able to explain all of this on the Day of Judgment?

Institutionally the church participates in the middle-class style of life by its dedication to the pursuit of material comforts. It begins new missions in areas where this consideration is a foregone conclusion. Locally and nationally its investment in property and building construction, contrasted with its investment in combating human misery, leaves no doubt in anyone's mind where the accent falls or what this suggests to the Christian regarding the use of his personal resources.

We baptize middle-class respectability. It is not that we quietly endorse middle-class virtues; we tend to equate these virtues with the righteousness of God. No matter how well we verbalize another theology, it is widely assumed that if one assents intellectually to the appropriate doctrines and goes to church, he can bring his respectable moralism into the church without any overhauling — or even any question. Far from helping him sense a radical new involvement in humanity, it may harden him against becoming sympathetic to those whose way of life seems inferior and whose morality is not as acceptable to the church. His middle-class virtues are widely admired in the church, so the vices of the poor may appear all the more abhorrent.

This obscures the fact that also middle-class virtues are under the judgment of God. Much of our preferred middle-class respectability is self-deceptive and especially conducive to the sin of pride. In the case of pregnancy out of wedlock, for example, a girl from the Lower East Side is much more apt to accept what has happened and to face it honestly than is a girl from fashionable Yonkers. The girl from Yonkers will be under considerable pressure to hide the deed, to seek an escape, and perhaps get an abortion. In such a case the mask is off. Middle-class morality is not seen as preferable or more righteous, after all. It is not necessarily an indication of greater evil in the Yonkers girl, but evidence that evil can be sophisticated; and when it is, it tends to be more deceptive and hence more demonic.

We teach our children false values. One of the greatest tragedies is that we condition our children against the Gospel by promoting

the middle-class style of life. We may say all the right things in
church and Sunday school, but the vision with which we shape our
children's future and help them dream dreams contradicts us. For
the most part parents would not receive it as a cause for joy if their
youngsters decided to live in the slums of a city or in some
underdeveloped country as servants of Christ. They would be
surprised — caught off guard — and thus reveal that they never
expected anything like that to happen all the time they were
teaching them the church's party line. They would be disappointed
and anxious, afraid something must be wrong, because their real
concern is that their children enjoy a respectable, self-indulgent
life. This reaction would further betray how, in foisting such
values upon our children, we are simply remaking them in our
image. Most parents do such a good job that the problem just
mentioned never arises. In short, despite our words to the contrary,
we do not really want our children to seek first the kingdom of God
and His righteousness, but the American way of life.

Such a style of life is a commitment to self-promotion, exclusion,
and evasion of human problems. It is self-promoting because it
places too high a value on our own comfort; it indicates an inordi-
nate desire for earthly possessions; and it is nourished by a search
for status. It is exclusive because in this style of life people of
similar background and circumstances are drawn together, like iron
filings by a magnet, into neighborhoods which have systematically
eliminated the less worthy. It is evasive because it cuts us off from
precisely those people whose needs are most acute and to whom the
Gospel recommends us most of all.

Albert Schweitzer said: "Whatever you have received more than
others in the way of health, in talents, in ability, in success, in
a pleasant childhood, in harmonious conditions of home life, all
this you must not take to yourself as a matter of course. You must
pay a price for it. You must render in return an unusually great
sacrifice of your life for other life."

Our Lord told a man: "Go, sell everything you have and give it to
the poor, and come and follow Me."

Being middle class and living middle class is not wrong; but are
we so heavily committed to the middle-class style of life that we

cannot even consider such proposals or search out their meaning
for us?

We Are Committed to a Success Theology

Our commitment to the middle class style of life has not been
made without a theological foundation. The theology which informs
our life is a theology occupied with success. Not that this success
theology is a carefully articulated one; it is not. For the most part it
operates on undeclared assumptions, such as the following:

> The church's goal as an institution is to grow. Stewardship means giving
> to the church. Loyalty to the church is loyalty to our Lord. The Kingdom
> can be built by willing hands. The priesthood of believers means pulling
> laymen out of the world to serve on church committees. Religion is
> a separate compartment of life, and the church's task is to enlarge that
> compartment.

Although these assumptions of our success theology are usually
undeclared, they find their most careful expression in journals of
practical theology and in materials distributed by district and
national offices of the church.

. In reality, two theologies exist side by side — the one, a Biblical
theology to which lip service is paid and which is hallowed in
weighty journals and on solemn occasions; the other, a theology of
success. The latter is the theology which controls our major decisions
and is therefore the real theology of the church. Evidence
surrounds us.

Budgets, mission goals, and building programs. "How come the
Holy Spirit calls so many seminary graduates to the suburbs?"
a colleague of mine asks in mock seriousness. The Holy Spirit is not
quite as preoccupied with the suburbs as we are, nor as unconcerned
about areas of poverty. A study of national church budgets rein-
forces the contention that we are much more interested in successful
ventures than in suffering, more wrapped up in buildings than in
people. National and regional mission goals presuppose that our
resources will be invested overwhelmingly in new, middle-class
developments where success can be calculated with impressive
exactness, so that within a given number of years the initial
investment will have been repaid, and from that time on the dollars
that flow in can be reinvested in other new developments, thus

continuing the cycle of success. If numbers of people and human
need were determining factors in mission expansion, drastic changes
would occur.

In the local congregation, too, our priorities are clear. The focus
of our investment has not failed to impress the rank and file.
Hence it is much easier to get large pledges for an unnecessary new
building than it is for world relief or for human rights or for mission-
ary personnel in underdeveloped areas at home or abroad. It is so
much easier, in fact, that few congregations even try to secure
more than token support for the latter. Where is the congregation
that decides *not* to erect a new building but instead to invest
$100,000 to plead the cause of migrant workers?

Colleges and seminaries. In the fall of 1964 announcements came
only a few days apart from two Lutheran colleges in Minnesota
indicating that expansion during the next decade for these two
schools would total $50 million. Perhaps persuasive reasons can be
given for this massive commitment, but it must be recognized as
massive. The excellence of these institutions is not in question, nor is
the contribution they have made and probably will make to the
church and to society. No doubt it is considerable. One can legiti-
mately question, however, whether such huge expenditures represent
an authentic understanding of the church in mission, always seeking
to press into the world and expend itself in love. Is this the church
caring for human need, or is it the church erecting glorious monu-
ments to itself? The question cannot be brushed aside. Suppose that
during the next 10 years my denomination invested $50 million in an
effort to give Negroes free access to housing wherever its members
now live. Can anyone doubt that this would represent a far more
significant witness to the world, a more convincing sign of life
within the church?

In a similar vein, it is difficult to assess the extent to which our
seminaries, by being comfort-minded for students and geographi-
cally remote from urban struggles, also partake of and encourage
a success theology.

Denominationalism. One facet of our success-mindedness is the
extent to which we are bent on perpetuating denominations. We
usually find ourselves in friendly competition with one another but

rarely in dialog. This situation can prevent us from discerning human need. Each major denomination rushes to plant a mission in a new suburban development, not because the people of that neighborhood would be left without the ministry of Word and Sacrament but in order to get in on the ground floor along with or ahead of the others. Of course, we rationalize such a practice by appealing to our confessional convictions. However, such a questionable motive is betrayed by the fact that there are countless neighborhoods of poor people in cities throughout the world and within our own country where numbers are so large and human need so extensive that there is no competition among the churches. But we are not worried about *their* denominational loyalty.

All these things spell out the story that instead of being God's instrument of service to the world we are *badly introverted*, curved in upon ourselves. We act as though Christ died for the church and not for the world, as though the church alone were the realm of His ruling activity, and as though our mission were therefore to the church. The institution and its programs become the focus and center of our religious activity. Our use of laymen to center their activities in the institution instead of the world may actually harden them against human need and make it possible for many of us to find religious sanction for being unresponsive toward and even self-righteous about a problem such as poverty.

A practical church journal publishes an article on "Social Welfare Checkup," dealing with a program for old people within the congregation. "What is *your* congregation doing to involve its older members meaningfully in the life and work of the church?" it asks. Another is entitled "The Unemployment Problem" and, predictably, has nothing to do with national unemployment — which probably never occurred to most of its readers as being a concern of the church anyway — but with getting more church members to serve on committees and become active. The article uses this little jingle:

Have your work well-planned,
Your plan well-manned,
Your man clear-brained,
And all God-sustained.

Perhaps more honestly than we would care to admit the jingle describes the working of our success theology. We make the plans and put them into operation—and expect God to sustain them.

This condition of being introverted or curved in upon ourselves is also manifestly a mode of *justification by works*. No matter what words we use to the contrary, we are in dead earnest to attain a success and a status of our own making. We are determined to justify our separate existence as members of a particular denomination. We are handing statistical reports to God, and we want them to be good.

The Church Must Die

It is not necessary that the church produce and live by a success theology. There is an alternative. The alternative to success theology is the theology of the cross. The theology of the cross is not a theology of failure; it is a theology of *apparent* failure, just as success theology is a theology of only apparent success.

The church must die. There is no other way to begin. "Unless a grain of wheat falls into the earth and dies, it remains alone, but if it dies, it bears much fruit." These words of Jesus before His crucifixion speak also to the church in its present misshapen form. They say that the church as an institution must die to itself, that we must recognize our commitment to the middle-class style of life as an idolatrous loyalty and confess our success theology to be in fact a heresy. To die this death means dying to everything that represents self-achievement before God and standing in the world— our lust for buildings, programs, and committees that promote the institution—for only if we so die can we be raised to life and bear fruit as the people of God.

The church that is willing to die will find resources for exciting new possibilities in the saving action of God. What are some of these resources?

The incarnation. The birth of the Savior proclaims that God has come to live with us in His Son, born in a small town of an outlying province of the empire, without even the warmth of a home and a bed. He went through the stages of embryonic development, was born of a virgin, and as an infant soon knew what it meant to be cold and hungry and afraid. He became a displaced person in Egypt, one of those misunderstood Jewish refugees. He came to be

our neighbor in the flesh, to share life with us — not to be aloof
from human need but to identify Himself completely and
unreservedly with the misery and agony and joy of man. If we learn
to see it this way, the manger is not a pretty decoration for
a Christmas service but a sign by which God calls us to let His love
take on flesh for the world today. Cancerous patients, unwed
mothers, hungry children — these become our burning concern.

Christ, the suffering Servant. Jesus was an offensive Messiah. He
didn't fit the bill at all. Nothing He did was very kingly. John the
Baptizer, who had publicly announced Him to be the Messiah, was
understandably disturbed. For all his efforts he sat alone and
ignored, a condemned man in Herod's prison, while Jesus, instead of
assuming kingship as the Messiah, was out in the country preaching
to groups of poor people and healing the sick. So John sent
messengers to Jesus to ask Him: "Are you the Messiah, or shall we
look for someone else?" Jesus answered them: "Go and tell John
what you have seen and heard: the blind receive their sight and the
lame walk, the lepers are cleansed and the deaf hear, the dead are
raised up, and the poor have the good news preached to them. *And
blessed is he who takes no offense at Me!*"

The puzzling ministry of Jesus among the poor and afflicted, which
had offended John, became precisely the evidence Jesus used to
attest to His being the Messiah. The Messiah must be the Servant, He
was saying, the suffering Servant who dies for the sins of the people.

The disciples of Jesus did not understand. Theirs too was a success
theology, against which Jesus asserted that "success" was to be
balanced on different scales. "Whoever would be great among you
must be your servant, and whoever would be first among you must
be your slave; even as the Son of Man came not to be served but to
serve and to give His life as a ransom for many."

So the church is to be the servant church. Wherever there are
people and wherever human need abounds, there the church is to
engage in its proper work, not of becoming a successful institution
but of serving the world unto death. In this framework our Lord's
description of the Last Judgment in Matthew 25 is overpowering.
There he has no time for year-end reports; he simply says: "I was
hungry and you fed Me. . . . I was naked and you clothed Me. . . .

I was a stranger and you took Me in." And he will explain: "As you did it to one of the least of these My brothers, you did it to Me."

The crucified and risen Lord. As the Christ, Jesus came not simply to be a good example but to die and rise again. By this momentous action God was making right the wrongs of mankind and offering us all His pardon. In a strange way God conquered the two unconquerable enemies of the human race: sin and death. He did so to create on earth a new community of His people, who would be alive in Him and bearers of His life to the world. Thus the church can, by baptismal participation in the death and resurrection of Jesus, receive the gift of God in Christ and become a new community of compassion in the world. It can, if it is willing to die with Christ and rise with Him to newness of life.

The church as the body of Christ. When our Lord was on earth His body could mean only one thing—His physical body. Following His ascension, however, when His followers began to invade the world, *they* became the body of Christ, the physical presence of the risen Christ on earth. As the church we today represent Him in the flesh to people. People cannot see Him or talk to Him except as they see Him and meet Him in us. The church is charged with the responsibility of completing the mission which our Lord gave us and reflecting with integrity the work of mercy which was His work on earth. To the extent that we do so, we are faithful to our calling as the body of Christ. To the extent that we turn our backs on human need, we do so at the terrifying cost of ceasing to be the body of Christ. "As the Father has sent Me, even so I send you." Jesus sends the church into the world as the Father sent Him into the world, and He has made it clear what our work is to be.

The church as the dwelling place of the Holy Spirit. God has not left us powerless. So that we may be His compassionate people on earth, He determined to dwell in us and reshape us. The Holy Spirit does not bring us to faith and then take a vacation. Though we may indeed ignore Him and frustrate His work in us, He constantly seeks to baptize us with power and love so that we may be the kind of servants He has called us to be. Today the Pentecostal movement, for all its excesses and limitations, is spreading among those who have been merely an annoyance to success-minded churches. Perhaps this is a sign from God that His patience is not unending and that we dare not long refuse Him who said: "Receive the Holy Spirit."

The Church as a part of God's creation. The church is related to the world in a positive way. "In the world but not of the world" is a misleading expression if it suggests withdrawal from humanity's burdens, and this would in fact negate the meaning of God's creative and redeeming work for the world. "If any man is in Christ, he is a new creation; old things have passed away; behold, all things have become new." The church, as an instrument of God's new creation, ought to be uniquely equipped to understand and relate properly to the world, which is also God's creation. The church is asked to understand every person and every thing through Christ, not apart from Him, and Christ has shown us what this means. Such a stance toward the world is not exploitative or indifferent or self-righteous, but a hopeful and compassionate one.

What I have been trying to say in outlining this theology is that the church has gone radically astray, and therefore the church as it now is must give itself up to be crucified in order to live as the body of Christ on earth. I am not kidding even a little in saying this, but simply taking the Bible seriously. In 1964 a book appeared under the title *Death and Birth of the Parish*, which meant to proclaim that very point. One reviewer, in writing what I am sure he thought was an endorsement, ended his review with these words: "You will be challenged by this nervous book to examine your program and perhaps to modify it." It is my emphatic assertion, however, that modifying the program is not enough. The patient is terminally ill, and fluffing the pillow will not revive him. The church must die to its present self if it is to rise and live with Christ.

Can the Gospel Be Discerned in Its Present Context?

Spelling out such a theology is nothing new, of course, and it will be argued that the church has always said these things with varying degrees of precision and regularity. We must, therefore, go on to ask the question: Can the Gospel be the Gospel in its present context? If we have endorsed unchristian commitments to the middle-class style of life and to a success theology, then the Gospel has been set within a framework of churchism that has gone drastically astray. Given this context, is it possible for the Gospel to speak to us as a Gospel of radical grace and discipleship?

Shortly before the World's Fair opened in New York an article appeared in *Arena* magazine. The writer was disturbed by the extravagance of the fair and by the churches' uncritical participation in it. He talked to representatives of eight of the nine religious pavilions. His questions went something like this:

"The display of wealth and technology at the fair underscores a striking disparity between the massive resources at our disposal and such things as the slums of our cities, the unemployed, and the 'have-nots' who comprise most of the world. Will you in any way be raising critical questions about this? Will there be any sort of prophetic voice against values which can amass such wealth, leave unsolved the issues of poverty and injustice to others, and remove faith to the outskirts of life?"

Some said that was beyond their scope. One paused for a moment, then whistled a "Wow!" Another said candidly, "Everyone's going to be too busy promoting his own cause to tackle something like that."

Christ's call to us includes concern for human justice and human need of every sort, in fact, a concern so revolutionary that it is supposed to find itself constantly in conflict with the world's values, precisely those values which were so widely honored at the fair; for the fair extolled the rich and comfortable life and ignored agonizing misery in our nation and in the world. It appeared that the church was baptizing the values upon which the fair was premised by its virtual silence about them, thus relegating the Gospel to a segment of life that does not interfere with our real ambitions, and thus also diluting any meaningful sense of discipleship to which the Gospel, properly presented, always calls us. But can the Gospel really be the Gospel if it comes along as conformity with the world rather than as judgment against its values?

We speak of brotherhood while living and worshiping without protest in neighborhoods where Negroes are not given free access. In this manner we remove our theology from the human struggle and thus detach it from reality.

We say elegant words about the priesthood of believers, but in

a context which makes clear that we really mean believers should do
more for the institution, not be concerned citizens and Christian
mechanics.

When a woman in an all-white neighborhood drives to church
(past three other churches) in a late-model car, wearing $80
worth of clothes, to sip tea from expensive china, and then packs
98 cents' worth of articles in relief kits and turns in a "mite box"
for missions, one may well ask if it is remotely possible for the
Gospel to be distinguished in all this or if it is rather a cheap
bargain with God for an easy conscience.

The morning mail brings 10 copies of 2 multicolored posters from
church headquarters. One shows what is evidently an all-white
congregation worshiping in a new church. The other shows a family
of five well-dressed Caucasians sitting in a spacious living room that
has large windows and modern furnishings. It clearly bespeaks
a substantial suburban home. The message on top says: "The Christ
of the cross loves all. . . . Bring your friends to church during
Lent." On the bottom it reads: "Christ is not to be contained — but
shared." The words speak — but the context also speaks and slants
the meaning of the words. In this way it is possible to substitute
slogans for understanding.

Church bodies officially publicize work in neighborhoods of
poverty and beg for funds to support such work, but when the
budget is examined for actual expenditures, it leads us to suspect
that we exploit poverty more than we minister to the poor. Meaning
is diluted in this context.

Where the church does find itself situated — not by design — in an
inner-city neighborhood, its entire orientation is such that it
inclines to retain its middle-class flavor and almost unavoidably
appeals to the joiners, the aspirers. After all, even in a bad
neighborhood one can hope to find some "nice" people. No
wonder, then, that churches are dying in the cities, because our
Lord never promised that the gates of hell would not prevail against
private religious clubs. Indeed, God may very well use the gates of
hell to topple such a perversion of the body of Christ.

Just as the church throughout its history has had a doctrine of the
Antichrist to designate pseudo-Christian pretensions concerning the

person and work of Christ, so today we need a doctrine of the anti-church—the church that masquerades as the body of Christ but in reality does not manifest the nature of His earthly presence.

During the Reformation period evangelical churches refuted the idea that the sacraments work ex *opere operato*, that is, automatically and apart from faith. Today Roman Catholic thinking is moving toward the same understanding. Ironically, we are not willing to reckon seriously with the fact that we have done precisely with the spoken Gospel what we deplored regarding the sacraments. We have widely assumed that a properly verbalized and orthodox theology automatically communicated what it was supposed to communicate, as though the context had no bearing on it. We have taken for granted that with complete integrity we can divorce ourselves from the problems of world poverty and in isolated splendor enjoy the comfort of the Gospel.

But the Gospel is no longer the Gospel in that context.

B. POVERTY AND THE CHURCH

Compassionate Involvement

The need is for Christians to express a kind of total involvement in the world, an involvement of compassion.

First the church has to rid itself of all pretensions, either about its past performance or about the ease with which it can now presume to be God's instrument of service in the world. The fact is that God has used other instruments to serve people, and often these "secular" instruments have been far more perceptive and courageous than the church in exposing and healing the sores of humanity. To go from a church council meeting or a pastoral conference to a civil rights assembly is often to see how much we have to repent of—how clever we are when it comes to our own rights and how cautious and careless when it comes to more urgent rights for others.

We have an unacknowledged responsibility for injustice others suffer. Today in America poverty, as an unnecessary suffering, is an injustice—an injustice deeply entangled with its other forms, notably racial prejudice.

Injustice has a way of putting us on one side of the fence or the other. Either in some way we are hurt by it or in some way we profit by it, although profiting by injustice is a shortsighted profiteering. By and large the readers of this book are among those who profit by it. Most Christians in America do. Let me use myself as an example.

The apartments I secured for our congregation's parish workers could not have been rented by Negroes. That was made clear to me. So in a very real sense we are living at their expense. Negroes are subjected to extra costs, restrictions, and humiliations in renting apartments on Ninth Street, and one immediate consequence was greater accessibility for our white staff.

The price we extort from Negroes in the matter of housing is multiplied — if more hidden — in the case of all-white neighborhoods, where acknowledged or unacknowledged restrictive agreements are in force (or would be, if there were any "threat"). Most of you who read this live in such neighborhoods. By your silence in going along with the system you may indeed preserve some artificial values, but that is just the point — you are enjoying the benefit of these artificial values at the price of injustice to others, in this instance the injustice of keeping Negroes in ghettos, in inferior but more expensive housing, as well as a host of other injustices that stem from this.

We know well enough what happens in a Caucasian congregation when members are asked to sign open-occupancy statements declaring their willingness, should the occasion arise, to sell or rent their homes to persons regardless of racial, ethnic, or religious background. In the instances with which I am familiar, only a handful out of hundreds do so. When this matter is discussed, someone is sure to express the feelings of many by saying: "What would my friends and neighbors think?" or: "Property values would go down and I'd lose money." To which it can be answered: Your friends and neighbors might think you meant business about being a Christian — indeed you might offend some. And if your Christian principles mean something only when they don't cost you, then get rid of them. Your principles are worth only what you are willing to pay for them, and if you are not willing to pay for them, they aren't worth a dime.

This illustrates how distorted the Gospel becomes when set into a false context. Peter tells us we should not be surprised when we are called upon to suffer for Christ, as though something strange were happening. Most church members count it not only strange, however, but ridiculous to think they should risk suffering.

How much of the money we have invested — or our church has invested — may in some way be reaping a profit off the squalid housing conditions in city slums? Who can know the ways we are entangled in a system which profits off the suffering of others?

Similar patterns could be discerned in education and employment as these affect the poor in general and the Negro poor in particular. But the evidence is stark enough. If Christians wish to be servants of Christ and if the church wishes to be His body, then we must prepare for an aggressive, compassionate involvement in the world.

Involvement will not come easily for Christians who have a strong churchly tradition of separation from anything political. We must therefore learn to recognize both the truth and the untruth in statements like "The church should keep out of politics" and "The church's job is to preach the Gospel." On the one hand, such expressions remind us that the church is not a political organization. It is not the church's task to offer top-minded pronouncements on all sorts of complex issues with which it is not technically competent to deal, much less lobby for its own institutional interests. Its proper function is to share the Gospel with the world.

We must go on to recognize, however, that as the earthly presence of Christ the church is called to penetrate every sphere of life with Christian compassion and understanding. Otherwise its proclamation of the Gospel is reduced to slogan-making. The church is called to *live* the Gospel *in* the world as well as to proclaim the Gospel to the world. Unless the Gospel takes on flesh and blood in human affairs of every sort, it will quite appropriately fall on skeptical ears — or even worse, on ears that are eager to hear their own complacency blessed.

Too often the refrain "Keep out of politics and preach the Gospel" has been an unkind excuse to be loveless and unresponsive to people. It can reflect a fierce impulse to divide life into separate "religious" and "nonreligious" compartments. It is frequently an attempt to restrict the Gospel to a context which will render it inoperative in critical areas of life. It may indicate that we have tried hard to contain Christian love in that important but limited sector of life we call personal piety, but have failed to recognize that personal piety often walks with an alter ego of corporate lovelessness, so that we are willing to be kind to people in direct, personal dealings, but not willing to love them by involving ourselves in corporate actions or decisions. As basic as it obviously is to share Christian love in personal relationships, we have to face the hard fact that we live in a society so complex that some of the most urgent needs of our fellowmen can be attended to only through responsible participation in labor unions, political organizations, PTA's, and the like. The poor in America today offer only one outstanding example of needs which cannot be met by private action alone. Personal piety standing aloof is at best inadequate and at worst hypocritical, and therefore our tradition of noninvolvement in anything political is seen to be unfaithful to the authority of the Bible, which it pretends to follow.

In the January 1965 issue of *Inner City*, a bimonthly newsletter for urban pastors, the following letter appeared from a Texas physician. It illustrates the assumptions that frequently accompany a theology of noninvolvement.

To the Editors of Inner City:

I have been a Lutheran all of my life and extremely proud of my choice because basically the Lutherans are a frugal, hard-working group of people that ask for nothing that they cannot produce. Then to see the statement attributed to you three exponents of the Lutheran faith asking the government to take care of the poverty situation and this brotherhood of man is beyond my possible conception.

Have you gentlemen lost faith in your God to the point that you expect Lyndon Johnson, Mr. Humphrey, and Mr. Goldwater to displace the charitable endeavors of the Lutheran Church? Do you really believe that the Lutherans of the United States need a law to establish the equality of man? If you do, then I suggest you search your soul and maybe some- where you will find a denomination that follows your precepts, and I can assure you it is not in the Lutheran faith.

Anyone who does not believe in the basic principles of Christ's charity and has to look to the government is in my books a "faker." I hate to see the likes of you infiltrate a religion as beautiful as Lutheranism.

The reply to this medical doctor read as follows:

Your letter begins by getting at just the two matters that ought to concern Christians above all others — the nature of the Gospel and the nature of the church. You have indicated your position on these with a rare display of honesty. While your assumptions are widely accepted within the institutional church, they nevertheless represent a perversion of the Good News.

Let's begin with the nature of the Gospel. St. John tells us that "in this is love, not that we loved God, but that He loved us and sent His Son to be the expiation for our sins." St. Paul writes that we are saved by grace through faith, "and this is not your own doing, it is the gift of God — not because of works, lest any man should boast." I wonder, therefore, if there is not something radically deficient in your opening remark, "I have been a Lutheran all of my life and extremely proud of my choice."

Now consider the nature of the church. Where the church is, there God's grace is the order of the day. By Him we are joined together, undeserving sinners all — prostitutes and pastors, dope addicts and doctors — in the fellowship of Christ's love. "There is neither Jew nor Greek, there is neither slave nor free, there is neither male nor female; for you are all one in Christ Jesus." I wonder, however, if you are impressed by this when you say you are proud of your choice to be a Lutheran, "because, basically, the Lutherans are a frugal, hard-working group of people that ask for nothing that they cannot produce." Your statement appears instead to reflect an image of the church as a prestigious religious club of like-minded people who are engaged in self-promoting virtues.

I wonder also if there is not an intimate connection between your pride in choosing a respectable religious institution and your understanding of poverty and brotherhood.

If salvation is not by grace, and if the church belongs to the deserving, then perhaps we have theological roots for restricting chari and limiting brotherhood. But if the church is the congregation of sinn who have received mercy, and if the church, as the body of Christ, is t bearer of God's mercy to the world, then we have a calling to let love invade every facet of life, also political life, and to labor so that no man is treated unjustly or robbed of his humanity. As you well know, in our nation not everyone enjoys the opportunity of fair and humane treatment, Texas being no notable exception.

Since government is an instrument of God meant for the temporal welfare of all people, Christians have a clear mandate to use this means in restraining the arm of the oppressor and promoting the cause of the oppressed. Law cannot produce love, but law can be an instrument of love, even when it enforces the lesser virtue of justice.

Do you really believe that Lutherans can, through private charity, adequately cope with the massive problem of poverty in America today? Do you think that churches can remain segregated and Christians allow the powers that be to endorse (by design or default) second-rate citizenship for Negroes and still speak with integrity about brotherhood?

If you are so convinced that private piety by itself is the answer, then I invite you to come and live in the slums of one of our cities or with the migrant workers of Texas, and there, in an act of holy foolishness, spend your years and your skills and your energy, not merely to bestow "charity" but to share yourself with fellow humans who must agonize through restrictions and problems that do not now touch you. And then — but only then — we will listen eagerly as you tell us why government is not an appropriate avenue for human concern, and how personal charity can do the job.

The tradition of noninvolvement is called by church historians "quietism." It has afflicted Lutheran piety (my tradition) with particular force, but also the Christian church in general. Quietism tends to make of Christianity an otherworldly religion that is eager to offer people heaven but does not direct itself aggressively to the problems of earth. It would have us believe that the only city worth exerting ourselves for is the City of God. And although this view commends no particular effort at bettering the lot of others, it invariably permits those holding the view to do well for themselves.

Quietism nurtures the idea that "politics is dirty" and Christians should keep out. If you wish to test the effectiveness with which this idea has caught hold, next time you admire an infant son of

Christian parents tell them, "Maybe he'll grow up to be a poli-
tician," and see for yourself what the reaction is. Quietism makes
church members more apt to write their elected officials about
hunting seasons and tax laws than about adequate provisions for
mental patients or rehabilitation of prisoners. Christian politicians
sometimes bemoan the fact that church conferences and ministeriums
are more vocal about bingo regulations than about discrimination in
housing and employment.

When my brother first became a member of the Illinois House of
Representatives he learned that although the state was 6 percent
Lutheran, only one half of one percent of those holding higher
public office were classified as Lutheran. That is one twelfth of
what across-the-board percentages might suggest as the "Lutheran
share" of responsibility. Of course, if we expect that Lutherans, as
Christians, should be more concerned than others with the welfare
of humans, the percentages show even greater disparity.

Quietism is strongly reflected in Christian hymns, many of which
betray an otherworldly theology which has little in common with
the Biblical witness. One searches almost in vain for hymns which
project the Christian life in a way that relates the Gospel to concrete deeds of love for others. Most of our hymns lack any meaningful expression of the Christian's work in the world. They tend to
convey a piety that separates religion from reality and therefore
to perpetuate a tradition of quietism. The world is very evil, and
we must cling to Jesus until He leads us to our heavenly home, runs
the theme. Such a theme has its place in Christian piety, and it
is especially understandable that hymns produced, for example,
against the background of the Thirty Years' War would return consistently to this theme. However, it is not a balanced theology, and
if we honestly want to let our liturgy be a momentous and joyful
celebration of Christ's victory, then we should also sing about
discipleship.

Quietism is not only a possible but a necessary counterpart of
preaching that is preoccupied with the question of personal salvation. When personal salvation alone becomes the goal of Christians, then nothing else matters very much once this goal has been
assured. The church can be viewed as the institutional guarantor of

that salvation and need not be understood as the living body of
Christ in which one's relationships to the world are determined. The
world in turn becomes not the arena of service but a way of life
that has nothing to do with religion. "Being saved" is seen as the
end, not the beginning, of God's work in us — and that explains
why the Holy Spirit is just an appendage to our thinking. Eternal
life is something that is stashed away for the hereafter, not
a present reality. In Sunday school one of the stock answers children
give to the question, "Why did Jesus die?" is, "So we can go to
heaven." For many Christians this is an accurate summary of the
salvation story.

Against this it is necessary to maintain that although Christianity is indeed "otherworldly," it is likewise "this-worldly," the
most this-worldly way of life on earth. Our whole understanding of
"last things" must be reorganized to take both aspects faithfully
into account.

Matthew has grouped the sayings of Jesus concerning the last
things into chapters 24 and 25. It is striking that at this very
point in which we might expect Jesus to be most otherworldly, he
surprises us by being the most worldly. It is the servants who use
their talents for their master while he is away who are properly
prepared at his return. The theme is driven home consistently that
those who have a proper hope in the future are those who busy
themselves with the work of the Master now — a work that is force-
fully pressed upon us: feeding the hungry, clothing the naked,
visiting the sick and imprisoned. We are to be compassionately involved in the world as our Lord was compassionately involved.

In the fourth gospel the same emphasis is driven home in John's
understanding of eternal life not as a future gift but as a present
reality ("He who believes *has* eternal life") and the inseparable
bond between life and love for the brother evident in the Gospel,
but even more impressively clear in the First Epistle of John.
St. Paul, too, links salvation with our present life in the Spirit, and
when he maintains (Ephesians 2) that salvation is a gift from God,
not a product of our works, he immediately adds: "For we are His
workmanship, created in Christ Jesus for good works. . . ."

I am only hinting at the massive evidence in both the Old and the New Testament which leads us to this conclusion: Any hope of heaven that does not drive one into a joyful, compassionate involvement in the world is a perversion of the Gospel of Jesus Christ. An otherworldly theology which seeks to escape the problems of life promotes an unacceptable worldliness because it surrenders to the world most of life and secures only one small sector, the religious sector, as the proper realm of God's concern. It lends integrity to the notion that the church is—and should be—out of touch with things that really count and that God is to be discerned on the surface of life, not in its depths.

For the most part American Christians have bought such a theology lock, stock, and barrel.

Now it is imperative that we return to the compassionate Christ and as His body on earth become compassionately involved in the world.

What Can We Do?

"But what can we do?" the question is asked. Perhaps the questioner means, "What little thing can I do to get off the hook?" Then the answer of course is, "Nothing"—which may be the answer he wants to hear. On the other hand, if the question is asked in utter seriousness, there is a good deal one can do. I hope I have made it abundantly clear that, first of all, it is not a matter of doing certain things but of *being* a certain kind of Christian and a certain kind of church. If one recognizes his *being* as a man in Christ, there is an astounding array of things that can be done.

First, we can get rid of our deplorable sense of superiority and condescension toward the poor. This comes to me in its crudest form when people say, "It's too bad your church isn't north of 14th Street with *our* kind of people." Or when they say, "You are certainly getting some good experience there!" implying that of course I will soon move on to greener pastures where the church *really* belongs. But it is also patently present in the "lady bountiful" attitude toward the poor and the "we must help those backward people" tone, which is often the unspoken pride we nourish in going through the motions of love. We must learn to know the poor as *people*, or we rob them of their humanity, the most precious earthly gift of God. We must see them as equals, not

equals in circumstance but equals in worth to God and to man, and
we must repent of every phony excuse which seems to justify a lesser
understanding. Reading can help a lot. James Baldwin, Martin
Luther King, William Stringfellow, and Michael Harrington are only
a few of many good possibilities.

Second, we can act to alleviate and eliminate poverty. For one
thing, we can become much more generous in sharing our personal
wealth with others. However, personal generosity is not enough in
our complicated world, and therefore we must see that God has
committed us to use government as a means of bettering the
earthly lot of others. Government is God's servant for human good,
Paul tells us, and we despise this function of government at the
peril of despising the poor. Let me make clear that I am not talking
about the government as a sort of super-Santa Claus that exists
apart from us, but I am talking about how we can assume responsibility for helping people become positive contributors to the world
and share with others the benefits of their contributions. I think
chapter 4 makes plain that I speak of taking people off welfare,
not putting them on. But doing so requires aggressive political
action on our part.

Third, we must never think that our ultimate goal is to make the
poor "unpoor." From the Christian point of view that is a shortsighted look at things. There is a real danger that we secretly
endorse for the poor the very things we pretend to deplore about
the idolizing of middle-class values. We could eliminate poverty,
and the church might still be as much, perhaps more, a perversion
of the body of Christ than it is now. The whole nation might be
a moral slum. We ought rather to see that there is no Christian
answer apart from living among the poor, sharing life with them,
and planting the Gospel among them. That is why in this chapter
I have not spoken about eliminating poverty apart from flesh-and-
blood efforts on our part to get the poor united with us as members
of the body of Christ. The salvation of God embodies a concern for
man's earthly wholeness, to be sure, but it never gets so stuck on
this that it loses sight of his eternal destiny. For this reason it
would be disastrous if we unwittingly perpetuated among the poor
the same parochial preoccupation with self that now characterizes

the institutional church. The poor must learn along with us — if we
are members one of another — that the Gospel calls us to look
beyond ourselves and to care about people. Thus the poor of our
land should never be made to feel as though they were the object of
the church's generosity but that we are all the object of God's
generosity, and all of us are alive to share that generosity with
others. The American Christian who is poor has the same relation
to the poor of the world that you and I may have to both of them.
So the Christian's stance toward poverty in America cannot be
detached from his stance toward the poor of the world. If we do
detach the two, we may wake up one day wealthier than ever, with
no poor in the nation, but so outrageously impoverished of concern
for others that the spirit of Christ cannot be recognized among us.
Therefore we must see that it is also human and Christian for the
poor in America to share with those who are by comparison less
fortunate than they.

Fourth, lives are needed. Lives are sorely needed that quietly
expose the wonder of God among men. We must go and live among
the poor, whoever and wherever they are. When for valid reasons
that cannot be done, we must understand that God still asks for
our lives, and so a comparable sacrifice is required. Today we do
not even begin to perceive this. The back cover of the latest issue of
my favorite journal of practical theology makes an appeal for
"sacrificial gifts!" (italics theirs). It asks us to think what an extra
10 cents a day from every member would bring in. "A dime a day
is not a suggested goal for anyone. Many of us could do much
more. The suggestion is made to impress upon us all the value of
setting a challenging commitment. . . ." I have little room to talk.
In speaking to suburban groups I used to point out how, if
80 people in a given congregation gave the equivalent of four
cigarets a day, that congregation could fully underwrite a young
parish volunteer working full time in an inner-city parish and
extend a hand of love to many deprived youngsters. I would often
use this illustration when preaching on the words of Jesus in
Mark 8: "If any man would come after Me, let him deny himself and
take up his cross and follow Me. For whoever would save his life
will lose it; and whoever loses his life for My sake and the Gospel's

will save it." I don't do this anymore — not because I realize how seldom congregations rise to such a "challenge," but because in the light of what Christ says it is blasphemy. Our Lord isn't asking for cigarets.

Fifth, we can learn to celebrate. We need to rediscover what it means to celebrate the victory of Christ with one another. Our Sunday morning worship must become for us a joyous family celebration of Christ's resurrection as we sing our noisy praise to God and share the Gospel of our Lord in spoken and sacramental Word. But let it be a thing of joy, and let us learn to celebrate as God's new community with all manner of men. We need to celebrate in the sanctuary, and we likewise need to discover the joy of celebrating the presence of Christ in the world. He is present there, if we will but perceive Him in others and recognize His lordship over all earthly things. Some congregations — like East Harlem Protestant Parish, St. John the Evangelist Lutheran Church in Brooklyn, and St. Agatha Roman Catholic Church in Chicago — are uncovering the excitement of being God's people and of linking a vital Sunday celebration with the neighborhood and the world that lies beyond the sanctuary doors. People awaken to find that ordinary things become extraordinary in Christ, and learn that daily activities can be a celebration of praise. They learn that being a Christian has to do with life and not just with religion, and so issues such as unemployment and slum housing and discrimination are seen not as unwelcome intrusions in the church but as a part of the guts of life to which the man of Christ must relate.

When I think of these things and of the church's future I am sometimes afraid. I am not afraid of the threat of world communism or of the resurgence of the non-Christian religions or of any persecution that conceivably may one day be unleashed upon the church. Of these I have no fear.

I am afraid when I think of hymn-singing Christians — Christians who sing praises to God on Sunday but who have no hankering to let Monday's work be a hymn of praise to God.

I am afraid of churchgoing Christians — Christians who go to church on Sunday, but for all the compassion they show toward the oppressed and forgotten poor might as well have stayed home.

I am afraid of praying Christians — Christians whose fine prayers are shot full of hypocrisy because they pray for the needy but reinforce the values that imprison the needy.

I am afraid for the church when I think of respectable Christians — Christians whose respectability will not permit them to take risks for those who are less respectable than they are.

I am afraid of such Christians because I know how easy it is for me to be such a Christian, and therefore I know how easy it is for you to be such a Christian.

There is no salvation for us apart from the Compassionate One, who let His body be broken for the purpose of uniting the human race in one great bond of love. But in the Compassionate One life has no meaning unless His compassion for the world becomes our passion.

This book was set, printed, and bound at Concordia Publishing House. Body type is 10/12 Spartan (Linofilm). Display type is Double Long Primer Antique. The book was printed offset on 60 lb. Mountie Eggshell paper. Photos for chapter openings and jacket are by Frank X. Mueller. Design is by Ted Smith.

Date Due

Demco 293-5